# THE

# SHEMITAH

# SOLUTION

## HOW TO POSITION YOURSELF IN THE YEAR OF THE LORD'S RELEASE

# TABLE OF CONTENTS

# INTRODUCTION

# THE WRITING IS ON THE WALL

*"He who dwells in the secret place of the Most High shall abide under the shadow of the Almighty. I will say of the LORD, He is my Refuge and my Fortress; My God, in Him I will trust. Surely He shall cover you from the snare of the fowler and from the perilous pestilence. He shall cover you with His feathers, and under His wings you shall take refuge; His truth shall be your shield and buckler. You shall not be afraid of the terror by night, nor of the arrow that flies by day, nor of the pestilence that walks in darkness, nor of the destruction that lays waste at noonday. A thousand may fall at your side and ten thousand at your right hand; but it shall not come near you. Only with your eyes shall you look, and see the reward of the wicked. Because you have made the LORD, who is my Refuge, Even the Most High, your dwelling place, no evil shall befall you, nor shall any plague come near your dwelling; For He shall give His angels charge over you, to keep you in all your ways".* (Psalm 91:1-11)

If you are reading this book it is likely that you have heard or learned at least something about the *"Shemitah"* year. A strange word, that has affected nations and generations since the beginning of creation. If you've heard about the *Shemitah* and understand its implications for this season then you may be uneasy or even uncertain about what lies ahead for you, your nation and the nations of the world. Even if you have not previously heard of this peculiar word *"shemitah,"* you're probably aware of how perilous the times are in which we live. When you consider the rise of ISIS, the spreading of Ebola, the saber rattling of Russia, the currency wars, the economic uncertainty, the increased racial and cultural tensions, you can probably see that the writing is on the wall. No doubt there is a convergence of political, economic, cultural, religious and social conflicts which is going to bring about some sort of transformation whether we are ready for it or not. So what do we do? Is there a solution and a plan? Is there a way to be secure during uncertain times? What should we do as followers of the Messiah, Jesus or Yeshua (His Hebrew name)?

Throughout this book I will reveal to you God's answers to these questions as they are found in Scripture. You will learn how to make the LORD your Refuge and Shield so that there is no need to fear pandemics, terror attacks, war or economic calamity. You will understand what to do and how you should live in a *Shemitah* Year or the Year of Release. Finally, by applying the information revealed in this book you will attract God's blessings to you, your family, community and city even in perilous times such as these.

As a matter of fact, if you do not feel the need to review foundational concepts of the Shemitah and are only interested in learning what we should do, you can skip right ahead to chapter four and begin reading there. Before you continue reading, I want to encourage you to again slowly read and internalize the previous passage from Psalm 91. Then, ask God to show you what to do to make this Word work on your behalf.

*"He who dwells in the secret place of the Most High shall abide under the shadow of the Almighty. I will say of the LORD, He is my Refuge and my Fortress; My God, in Him I will trust. Surely He shall cover you from the snare of the fowler and from the perilous pestilence. He shall cover you with His feathers, and under His wings you shall take refuge; His truth shall be your shield and buckler. You shall not be afraid of the terror by night, nor of the arrow that flies by day, nor of pestilence that walks in darkness,*

*nor the destruction that lays waste at noonday. A thousand may fall at your side and ten thousand at your right hand; but it shall not come near you. Only with your eyes shall you look, and see the reward of the wicked. Because you have made the LORD, who is my Refuge, Even the Most High, your dwelling place, no evil shall befall you, nor shall any plague come near your dwelling; For He shall give His angels charge over you, to keep you in all your ways".*
(Psalm 91:1-11)

# CHAPTER 1

# UNDERSTANDING GOD'S APPOINTMENTS

*"To everything there is a season, a time for every purpose under heaven..."* (Ecclesiastes 3:1)

Before you can truly benefit from any knowledge or information, whether it be from man or from God, it is critical that you understand the correct timing for applying the knowledge you have been given. This, by the way, is part of the definition of wisdom. Wisdom is not just having knowledge, but it is a skillful use and application of the knowledge one possesses. What good is the knowledge one has if he does not know how or when to apply it? While under the inspiration of the Holy Spirit, one of the wisest men who ever lived wrote: *"... Therefore get wisdom. And in all your getting get understanding."* (Proverbs 4:7) In this context, King Solomon spoke of the concept of true wisdom, being so closely related to the concept of understanding, that he admonished us to seek them together. The word translated as "understanding" is the Hebrew word *"biynah"* which is a reference to a kind of timely discernment or perception held by a person of wisdom. To put it simply, having wisdom gives one valuable insight on what to do at certain times that others without this wisdom or access to it are lacking.

Can you imagine having the insight to know not only how, but when to invest in certain things? How valuable would it have been to know beforehand about a collapse or shift in the market? How valuable would it be to know what investments would exponentially rise over the next few months? How beneficial would it be to know for certain what will happen in the days, months and years ahead?

While some would consider this type of insight to be prophetic in nature, I would very strongly defend that this type of insight is just as much the benefit and fruit of wisdom, as it is a benefit of prophecy. Wisdom as we discussed earlier is making a skillful application of knowledge, which will bring forth good fruits and success. Prophesy, which is from the Hebrew word *"navi"* (נביא)

is formed from the letters *nun* (נ), which is a picture of a seed,

and *vet* (ב) which is a picture of a house. Combine these two letters and it creates a pictograph of that which is housed in a seed. What is housed in seed you ask? Fruit! This means that the benefit of prophesy is that it reveals what fruit is coming forth. Also like wisdom, prophesy is time specific as it deals with the fate of individuals and nations.

# WISDOM TO DISCERN THE TIMES

*"And of the sons of Issachar who had understanding of the times, to know what Israel ought to do, their chiefs were two hundred; and all their brethren were at their command."* (1 Chronicles 12:32)

There is an old saying that says "timing is everything." If not taken out of context, this statement contains a great truth: everything has a specific timing for its purpose to be fulfilled. The passage above speaks of a particular group of Hebrew people, the sons of Issachar, who not only understood this truth, but sought to become very wise and skilled in understanding the times. The word translated as understanding in this passage, is the same word we described previously. The word is *"biynah"* and again, it refers to a timely discernment. In this context or passage the use of *biynah*, becomes even more significant when we understand the word translated as *times*. The word *"eth"* (עֵת), means *times*. However, when we look at the pictograph from the ancient Hebrew spelling of this word, the specific type of *times* they were skilled in discerning becomes even clearer. What is the ancient pictograph? The *ayin* (עַ) is a picture of an eye and represents seeing, and the *tav* (ת) is a picture of a sign or covenant mark. Combined, these letters create a pictograph of seeing or watching for the signs of the covenant. This means that the sons of Issachar were very skilled, particularly in discerning the special times of the covenant between God and His people.

# WHAT ARE THE COVENANT TIMES?

"And the LORD spoke to Moses, saying, speak to the children of Israel, and say to them; The feasts of the LORD, which you shall proclaim to be holy convocations, these are my feasts." (Leviticus 23:1-2)

Leviticus 23 is a chapter that has been mostly overlooked and not really taught on in modern times. It has generally been taught as a chapter that explains certain religious practices that God had ordained ONLY for the Jews before the coming of the Messiah. As such, this chapter and its contents have been written off as irrelevant and non-applicable historical information at best. Is that an accurate understanding of this chapter? Are the feasts spoken of just for the Jews of the Old Testament? Or can there be more meaning? Could these special events the Bible calls feasts also have meaning for us? Is it possible that understanding these feasts could give us a greater understanding and discernment for what to do during certain times, as it was said of the sons of Issachar? Furthermore, what are the Feasts spoken of in Scripture?

First, let's deal with the idea of these feasts being only relevant to the Jews of the Old Testament. In the Scripture above God does not say that these are feasts that only belong to and are to be observed by the Jewish people. Contrary to some church theology, God says that these are not Jewish feasts, but feasts of the LORD God. In other words, God says before He even lists what the feasts are, that they are His. Specifically, it reads *"...The feasts of the LORD, which you shall proclaim to be holy convocations, these are **MY FEASTS.**"* (Leviticus 23:2 *emphasis added).

Although for some, there may still seem to be a discrepancy because God instructs Moses to speak of these feasts to the children of Israel. Doesn't that statement make these feasts for the people of Israel? Well, yes. However, who are the children of Israel? Are they just the descendants of the sons of Jacob who God renamed Israel? Let's look to see how God defines "Children of Israel" in Scripture:

*"...For they are not all Israel who are of Israel, nor are they all children because they are the seed of Abraham; but, in Isaac your seed shall be called. That is, those who are the children of the flesh, these are not the children of God, but the children of the promise are counted as the seed."* (Romans 9:6b-8)

*"And if you are Christ's, then you are Abraham's seed, and heirs according to the promise."* (Galatians 3:29)

*"Therefore remember that you, once Gentiles in the flesh- who are called Uncircumcision by what is called the Circumcision made in the flesh by hands- that at that time you were without Christ, being aliens from the commonwealth of Israel and strangers from the covenants of promise, having no hope and without God in the world. But now in Christ Jesus you who once were far off have been brought near by the blood of Christ... Now, therefore, you are no longer strangers, but fellow citizens with the saints and members of the household of God."* (Ephesians 2:11-19)

# THE TRUE CHILDREN OF ABRAHAM

From these few passages, we can understand who the true children of Israel (or royalty with God) are. They are the seed of Abraham, not of the flesh, but the children of promise, those who are in Christ the Messiah.

Now I'm not sure if that made it clear to you that these feasts, holidays, etc., are not just for Jews or belong to the Jews. Nonetheless, in case you need more convincing, I want to encourage you to read Zechariah 14:16-17, which explains that even during the millennial reign, when the Messiah is reigning as King over all the Earth, that those left remaining of the nations will be required to celebrate, or observe, the Feasts of Tabernacles (one of the LORD'S feasts). Otherwise, they will not receive rain. This also supports the idea that the feasts are not just something that were relevant only before the Messiah came, but they will also have significance after the Messiah's first and second coming.

# WHAT ARE THE FEASTS?

"... The feasts of the LORD, which you shall proclaim to be holy convocations, these are My feasts." (Leviticus 23:1)

Before I explain what the feasts are let me just say that it is not my objective in this book to give a very detailed explanation of each feast, but set you on a course to seek to understand their relevance to us today. Now, let's take a look at the word translated as *feasts* in Leviticus 23. Interestingly, the word translated as *feast* does not mean feast at all.

This is actually an example of where not translating accurately directly from the Hebrew caused many to misunderstand something of great significance in the eyes of God. What is the word translated here? It is the word *"moed"* (מוֹעֵד) or *"moedim"* in the plural sense and it refers to divinely appointed times and seasons. It is from the root word *"ed"* (עֵד), which in the ancient Hebrew script forms a pictograph of seeing in the door. In other words, these *moedim* or divinely appointed times are times where God's people are granted greater access to God's presence and greater insight into His divine plan. This also means that *not* understanding or observing these divine appointments can cause us to miss God's plan for us in a particular season.

It was for this reason that the sons of Issachar were considered leaders amongst the children of Israel. They kept watch over and observed important covenant times between God and His people, and as a result knew what God's people were to do during these times (1 Chronicles 12:32). These wise men and leaders would have been aware of God's plan during appointed times and seasons. As a matter of fact, when you understand who the sons of Issachar were and their particular skill set, you will be clear that the wise men who came from the east to see Jesus (*Yeshua*) after his birth, were none other than sons of Issachar. (Matthew 2:1-2)

# HOW THE SONS OF ISSACHAR DISCERNED THE TIME OF CHRIST

*"To everything there is a season, a time for every purpose under the heaven: A time to be born, and a time to die;"* (Ecclesiastes 3:1-2)

How did the sons of Issachar discern when the Messiah was born? There are a couple of things you may need to understand to make this a bit clearer. Now the foundation is laid for understanding that the sons of Issachar were skilled in discerning the covenant times of God and His people. Yet, we have not discussed how they discerned these divine covenant times. How did they discern these times? To answer this question we will need to go all the way back the beginning and look closely at a passage of Scripture found in the first chapter of Genesis. The passage is Genesis 1:14-15 and I want to encourage you to read it carefully:

*"Then God said, let there be lights in the firmament of the heavens to divide the day from the night; and let them be for signs and seasons, and for days and years; and let them be for lights in the firmament of the heavens to give light on the earth; and it was so."*(Genesis 1:14-15)

This passage seems to simply explain that God made the stars, moon and cosmic lights. However, in it lays the key to understanding how the sons of Issachar not only discerned the times, but actually knew when Yeshua was born. As we've done before, we will take a closer look at a couple of words in the biblical Hebrew, which will give us the understanding we seek. The first word we'll examine is the word translated as *"signs."* It is the Hebrew word *"ot"* (אֹות) and although it means sign, the word actually refers to something miraculous. As such, an *"ot"* refers specifically to a type of miraculous sign, or an unusual occurrence or event. Now keep this in mind as we examine the next word in the previously mentioned passage, which will help us to understand how one discerns divinely appointed times.

# SIGNALS OF MIRACULOUS SEASONS

According to what we have read in Genesis 1:14-15, after having properly defined the word "signs," we now understand that God said that the lights in the heavens are also a signal to us of miraculous seasons, days and occurrences. Now, is there a better interpretation of the word *seasons*? Or is the *seasons* spoken of here strictly referring to fall, winter, spring and summer? As you probably guessed, the word translated seasons here, does have a different interpretation than what you may have known. The biblical word used here is *"moedim,"* the same word we discussed earlier, which refers to divine appointments or significant covenant times between God and His people. Now you see that understanding the two words translated in Genesis 1:14 (signs & seasons) allows you to have a different perspective and more accurate translation of this verse. The following is how this Scripture reads with this new understanding:

*"Then God said, let there be lights in the firmament of the heavens to divide the day from the night; and let them be for signals of*

*miraculous events and divinely appointed covenant times, and for days and years..."* (Genesis 1:14)

Hopefully, by now you understand how and why the sons of Issachar were so skilled in discerning what to do during covenant times. Clearly, they established themselves to understand the significance of the position of the stars and the moon during the *moedim* or divinely appointed times. As a matter of fact, do you remember what the "wise men" from the East said to Herod about how they knew the Messiah had been born? *"Where is He who has been born King of the Jews? For we have seen His star in the East and have come to worship Him."* (Matthew 2:2) These wise men knew the time of the first coming, because they understood from Genesis 1:14, that they were to be observant of miraculous signals from the heavens during the *moedim*.

# A WISE MAN DISCERNS THE TIME

*"... a wise man's heart discerns both time and judgment, because for every matter there is a time and judgment."* (Ecclesiastes 8:5-6)

So who were these "wise men" from the East? Were they Gentiles, who understood mysteries of the Kingdom? Consider this, Israel was once in captivity to Babylon, which is east of Jerusalem, and many of the children of Israel decided to remain in Babylon after their 70 years of captivity had ended. Moreover, some of the greatest scholars of Torah learning arose out of Babylon. Also, consider that amongst those Jewish Torah scholars living in Babylon there were a group who specialized in discerning divinely appointed times. It's likely that these wise men were descendants of the same "wise men" spoken of in 1 Chronicles 12:32, who could discern the appointed times of the Kingdom.

Somehow, over the course of history, these Feasts or appointed times lost significance and became concepts which many ignored. However, Yeshua did not think these *moedim* of God were irrelevant. As a matter of fact, Yeshua actually rebuked the Pharisees and Sadducees because they had the ability to predict the weather, by reading the skies, but could not discern the appointed times of God. (Matthew 16:3)

This leads me to ask a question. If Yeshua rebuked the Pharisees and Sadducees, because they could not discern the appointed times of God, then do you think it is also important for us to be able to discern the God's holy-dates and their present day significance? I will not take time in this work to explain in further detail how the *moedim* became misunderstood and disregarded by God's people, that is for another discussion. Nevertheless, I would like to identify for you the divinely appointed times or *moedim* as they are listed in Scripture. I believe that understanding the *moedim* is critical and foundational to having a good understanding of the Shemitah Year and therefore what we should do during a Shemitah Year.

# DIVINE DAYS AND DATES

*"And the LORD spoke to Moses, saying, speak to the children of Israel, and say to them, the feasts of the LORD, which you shall proclaim to be holy convocations, these are My feasts."* (Leviticus 23:1-2)

It is important to know that before you can truly comprehend the divinely appointed days of the LORD, you must understand that these dates and days do not correspond to man's calendar, but rather relate to God's calendar. Interestingly, often times when Christians are approached with the topic of divinely appointed days and times they respond as if God's holy days are insignificant or pagan in nature. However, the truth is the calendar that most of the western world follows is the one that is actually comprised of idolatrous beliefs. For example, have you ever considered the origin of the names of the days, weeks and months of the year? In the scriptures the only day of the week that is referred to by a name is the seventh day, which is called the Sabbath. So where did the names of the days and months come from? If you are curious, and you should be, I have listed the origin of the names below.

# THE DAYS OF THE WEEK

| SUNDAY | From the latin "dies solis", which means "day of the sun." This day was renamed after the sun god. |
| --- | --- |
| MONDAY | From the Anglo- Saxon "monandaeg," which means "the moon's day." This day was named after the goddess of the moon. |
| TUESDAY | Named after the Norse god Tyr, who was a god of war. |
| WEDNESDAY | Named after the Norse chief god Wodan or Odin (the father of Thor). |
| THURSDAY | Named after the Norse god Thor (the same Thor depicted in modern super hero movies). This |

| | |
|---|---|
| | day was called Thor's day. |
| FRIDAY | Named after the Norse Frigg, goddess of the clouds, the sky and marital love. She was the wife of Odin. |
| SATURDAY | Called "Saturn's day," named after the Roman god, Saturn, the god of agriculture. |

# NAMES OF THE MONTHS OF THE YEAR

Originally the Roman calendar only listed 10 months of the year. Nevertheless here are the months and the pagan gods after which they are named:

| | |
|---|---|
| JANUARY | Named after Janus, the Roman god of gates and doorways. |
| FEBRUARY | Named after Februa, which was the pagan Roman festival of purification. |
| MARCH | Named after "Mars," the Roman God of war. It was the first month of the earliest Roman calendar. |
| APRIL | Named after the Greek goddess Aphrodite, who was worshiped as the goddess of love and beauty. |

| | |
|---|---|
| MAY | Named after Maia, the Greek goddess of Spring. |
| JUNE | Named after Juno, the Roman goddess of marriage and the well- being of women. She was thought of as the wife and sister of Jupiter. |
| JULY | Named after Julius Ceasar who reformed the Roman calendar |
| AUGUST | Named after Augustus Ceasar. |
| SEPTEMBER | Named after the Latin *"septem,"* which means seven. |
| OCTOBER | Named after the Latin "octo",meaning eight and refers to the eighth month. |
| NOVEMBER | Named after the Latin word *"novembris,"* meaning "ninth month." |
| DECEMBER | Named after the Latin word *"December"*, meaning "tenth month." |

Now you can see with your own eyes and are encouraged to do additional research to understand not only the origin, but the historical significance of these pagan gods after which the days and months are named. Yet, regardless of what you discover, here are a few things God has said about His people associating with idolatry.

- *"You shall have no other gods before Me. You shall not make for yourself a carved image –any likeness of anything that is in heaven above, or that is in the earth beneath, or that is in the water under the earth; you shall not bow down to them nor serve them. For I, the LORD you God, am a jealous God, visiting the iniquity of the fathers upon the children to the third and fourth generations of those who hate Me, but showing mercy to thousands, to those who love Me and keep My commandments."* (Deuteronomy 5:7-9)

- *"You shall utterly destroy all the places where the nations which you shall dispossess served their gods, on the high mountains and on the hills and under every green tree. And you shall destroy their altars, break their sacred pillars, and burn their wood images with fire; you shall cut down the carved images of their gods and destroy their names from that place. <u>You shall not worship the LORD your God with such things.</u>"* (Deuteronomy 12:2-4 *emphasis added)

- *"Therefore my beloved, flee from idolatry… You cannot drink the cup of the LORD and the cup of demons; you cannot partake of the LORD's table and of the table of demons. Or do we provoke the LORD to jealousy? Are we stronger than He?"* (1 Corinthians 10:14, 21-22)

- *"And in all that I have said to you, be circumspect and make no mention of the name of other gods, nor let it be heard from your mouth."* (Exodus 23:13)

# SETTING DATES BASED ON IDOLATRY

*"... For what fellowship has righteousness with lawlessness? And what communion has light with darkness? And what accord has Christ with Belial? Or what part has a believer with an unbeliever?"* (2 Corinthians 6:14-15)

The point of this brief list and history of the origins of various days and times of the year is not to show how much idolatry has influenced our nations, but to help people understand how much idolatry has altered our understanding of God's calendar and divine appointments. However, don't be mistaken in thinking that this is just some small mishap. It most certainly is not. Do you think it just coincidence that most Christians including Church leaders are unaware of the significance of *moedim* (God's divine appointments)? Of course not, this was no accident.

Satan understood that if God's people don't know or understand God's divine appointments that they are not as likely to know what to do (1 Chronicles 16:32). This isn't a new strategy of the enemy. Do you remember Yeshua rebuking the Pharisees and Sadducees for being able to discern the weather but not the signs of the times (Matthew 16:3)? To be sure, Satan wants God's people ignorant of the timing of God's divine appointments. As a matter of fact, listen to what the Scripture says regarding the Anti-Christ's strategy to overcome God's people: *"He shall speak pompous words against the Most High, and shall intend to change times and law, then the saints shall be given into his hand for a time and times and half a time"* (Daniel 7:25).

Did you catch that? The plan of the Antichrists is to change <u>TIMES</u> and law. The word here translated as "times" is the Hebrew word *"zeman"* (זְמָן) which means "appointed occasions and seasons." In other words, the strategy of the enemy to get a hand up on God's people is to change or alter their knowledge or understanding of God's appointed times. For example, nowhere in the Word of God is Easter mentioned in Scripture in reference to the crucifixion and resurrection of the Messiah. The name Easter, if you have ever wondered, is actually of Babylonian (Aramaic) origin. Easter is the western translation of "Ishtar", who was the most important goddess of Babylonian times. She was thought of as the goddess of war, sex and fertility, whose symbols were the egg and bunnies.

So, if you've ever questioned why some Christians promote the resurrection of Christ with symbols of rabbits and eggs, now you have your answer. The enemy has changed and altered most people's understanding of divine appointed occasions (Daniel 7:25), to the point where most Christians have renamed one of God's most important seasons after a fertility goddess (Easter/Ishtar) and no longer refer to as the season of Passover (God's given name). Now let's examine the basics and identify God's divine appointments as they are listed in Scripture.

# GOD'S DIVINE APPOINTMENTS AND OCCASIONS

*"And the LORD spoke to Moses, saying, speak to the children of Israel, and say to them; The feasts of the LORD, which you shall proclaim to be holy convocations, these are My feasts."* (Leviticus 23:1-2)

**THE (Weekly) SABBATH DAY (SHABBAT)** – *"Six days shall work be done, but the seventh day is a Sabbath of solemn rest, a holy convocation. You shall do not work on it; it is the Sabbath of the LORD in all your dwellings."* (Leviticus 23:3)

*"Remember the Sabbath day, to keep it holy. Six days you shall labor and do all your work, but the seventh day is a Sabbath of the LORD your God. In it you shall do no work; you, nor your son, nor your daughter; nor your male servant, nor your female servant, nor your cattle, nor your stranger who is within your gates. For in six days the LORD made the heavens and the earth, the sea, and all that is in them, and rested the seventh day. Therefore the LORD blessed the Sabbath day and hallowed it."* (Exodus 20:8-11)

**PASSOVER (PESACH)** – *"On the fourteenth day of the first month at twilight is the LORD's Passover."* (Leviticus 23:5)

**THE FEAST OF UNLEAVENED BREAD (CHAG HA MATZAH)** – *"And on the fifteenth day of the same month is the Feast of Unleavened Bread to the LORD; seven days you must eat unleavened bread."* (Leviticus 23:6)

**THE FEAST OF FIRST FRUITS** – *"Speak to the children of Israel, and say to them, when you come into the land which I give to you, and reap its harvest, then you shall bring a sheaf of the first fruits of your harvest to the priest. He shall wave the sheaf before the LORD to be accepted on your behalf; on the day after the Sabbath the priest shall wave it."* (Leviticus 23:10-11)

**THE FEAST OF WEEKS (SHAVUOT)** – *"And you shall count for yourselves from the day after the Sabbath, from the day that you brought the sheaf of the wave offering: seven Sabbaths shall be completed. Count fifty days to the day after the seventh Sabbath; then you shall offer a new grain offering to the LORD."* (Leviticus 23:15-16)

**THE FEAST OF TRUMPETS (ROSH HA SHANNAH)** – *"Speak to the children of Israel, saying: in the seventh month, on the first day of the month, you shall have a Sabbath-rest, a memorial of blowing of trumpets, a holy convocation."* (Leviticus 23:24)

**THE DAY OF ATTONEMNENT (YOM KIPPUR)** – *"Also, the tenth day of this seventh month, shall be the Day of Atonement. It shall be a holy convocation for you..."* (Leviticus 23:28)

**THE FEAST OF TABERNACLES (SUKKOT)** – *"Speak to the children of Israel, saying: The fifteenth day of the seventh month*

*shall be the Feast of Tabernacles for seven days to the LORD."*
(Leviticus 23:34)

**THE SABBATH YEAR (THE SHEMITAH YEAR)** – *"Speak to the children of Israel, and say to them: when you come into the land which I give you, then the land shall keep a Sabbath to the LORD. Six years you shall sow your field, and six years you shall prune your vineyard, and gather its fruit: but in the seventh year there shall be a Sabbath of solemn rest for the land, a Sabbath to the LORD, you shall neither sow your field nor prune your vineyard."*
(Leviticus 23:2-4)

**THE YEAR OF JUBILEE** – *"And you shall count seven Sabbaths of years for yourself, seven times seven years; and the time of the seventh Sabbaths of years shall be to you forty- nine years. Then you shall cause the trumpet of Jubilee to sound on the tenth day of the seventh month; on the Day of Atonement you shall make the trumpet to sound throughout all your land. And you shall consecrate the fiftieth year, and proclaim liberty throughout all the land to all its inhabitants. It shall be a Jubilee for you; and each of you shall return to his possession, and each of you shall return to his family."* (Leviticus 25:8-10)

The divine appointed days listed above are all very significant in their own way. Each one holds a key to understanding some of the mysteries of God for every generation. So we could easily sidetrack and talk about the significance and prophetic implications of them all, but for the purpose of this work we will only discuss the significance and relevance of the one referred to as the Shemitah Year (also known as a year of release).

# CHAPTER 2

# ANALYZING THE SHEMITAH YEAR

*"At the end of every seven years you shall grant a release of debts."*
(Deuteronomy 15:1)

There are of course several main texts that you must be familiar with to begin to understand the significance of a Shemitah Year. One of those texts is the previous scripture listed above, which requires there to be a release of debts at the end of every seven years. The Hebrew word, which is translated here as "release", is the word *"shemitah"* which refers to a remission of debt or a suspension of labor, but it also means "to throw down" or "a shaking." It is a year where agricultural labor is suspended and no one is allowed to harvest what grows in the field. Whatever grows in the field, the Scripture says, is for everyone, including the animals. Look at what God says about the Shemitah Year in the Scriptures below:

*"And this is the form of the release: Every creditor who has lent anything to his neighbor shall release it; he shall not require it of his neighbor or his brother, because it is called the LORD's release."*
(Deuteronomy 15:2)


*"Six years you shall sow your field, and six years you shall prune your vineyard, and gather its fruit; but in the seventh year there shall be a Sabbath of solemn rest for the land, a Sabbath to the LORD, you shall neither sow your field nor prune your vineyard.*

*What grows of its own accord of your harvest you shall not reap,
nor gather the grapes of your untended vine, for it is a year of rest
for the land. And the Sabbath produce of the land shall be food for
you: for you, for your male and female servants, your hired man,
and the stranger who dwells with you, for your livestock and the
beasts that are in your land – all its produce shall be for food."*
(Leviticus 25:3-7)

From the previous scripture we see that the Shemitah Year was a
year where people were compelled to walk by faith. If someone
owed you money, which you probably counted on, you were
expected to release them from being indebted to you. You were
urged to forgive their loan and forgo any expectations of being
repaid by man. Instead, you were to look to God to take care of
you and even compensate you for what monies you may have
lost in relinquishing debts. However, that's not all. In being
prohibited from sowing or harvesting your fields, you would
have no natural plan or expectation for how you were going to
provide for yourself and your family. This is why the Shemitah is
a year of walking by faith like no other. From where would our
provisions come? If we canceled debts that are legitimately
owed to us and we don't plant or harvest our fields, what type of
livelihood could we have?

# A YEAR OF TRUSTING GOD WILL PROVIDE

*"But He answered and said. It is written, Man shall not live by
bread alone, but by every word that proceeds from the mouth of
God." (Matthew 4:4)*

The Shemitah Year is when mankind can truly see that man does not live by bread alone, but is sustained by the Word of Almighty God. (Matthew 4:4) It is a year when one has to resolve that no matter what things look like in the natural, God will take care of him or her. Look at how Yeshua encouraged His disciples to trust in God's care and provision for them:

*"Therefore I say to you, do not worry about your life, what you will eat or what you will drink; nor about your body, what you will put on. Is not life more than food and the body more than clothing? Look at the birds of the air, for they neither sow nor reap nor gather into barns; yet your heavenly Father feeds them. Are you not of more value than they? Which of you by worrying can add one cubit to his stature? So why do you worry about clothing? Consider the lilies of the field, how they grow: they neither toil nor spin; and yet I say to you that even Solomon in all his glory was not arrayed like one of these. Now if God so clothes the grass of the field, which today is and tomorrow is thrown in to the oven, will He not much more clothe you, O you of little faith? Therefore do now worry, saying, what shall we eat? Or what shall we drink? Or what shall we wear? For after all these things the Gentiles seek. For your Heavenly Father knows that you need all these things. But seek first the Kingdom of God and His righteousness, and all these things shall be added to you. Therefore do not worry about tomorrow, for tomorrow will worry about its own things. Sufficient for the day is its own trouble."* (Matthew 6:25-34)

## AN ECHO FROM GOD

It is interesting that these words of Yeshua to His disciples sound like an echo from God to Israel regarding His promise to provide for them during a Shemitah Year. I'm not sure if Yeshua made the previous statement during a Shemitah Year, but if He did the crowds hearing Him would have been reminded of God's promise of provision especially during a Shemitah Year. Let's take a look at what God says to Israel regarding not worrying about necessities during the seventh year:

*"So you shall observe My statutes and keep My judgments, and perform them; and you will dwell in the land in safety. Then the land will yield its fruit, and you will eat your fill, and dwell there in safety. And if you say, what shall we eat in the seventh year, since we shall not sow nor gather in our produce? Then I will command My blessing on you in the sixth year, and it will bring forth produce enough for three years. And you shall sow in the eighth year, and eat old produce until the ninth year; until its produce comes in, you shall eat of the old harvest."* (Leviticus 25:18-22)

# THE BLESSING OF THE SHEMITAH

*"Then the land will yield its fruit, and you will eat your fill, and dwell there in safety... Then I will command y blessing on you in the sixth year, and it will bring forth produce enough for three years."* (Leviticus 25:19,21)

It is remarkable that both of these passages of Scripture encourage God's people to trust Him for provision and safety. They implore them to rely upon Him and not their own strategy or abilities for survival. They both reiterate the promise of the Sabbath, that if we take time to rest from our labors and seek to do good deeds, we will not lack the things we need. In Leviticus, God actually promises His people that if they properly observe the Shemitah Year's mandates that He would cause such a great harvest to be reaped from the sixth year that it would last until the ninth year. So in this sense, the Shemitah Year is a year of great blessing. We are to be relieved of debt and burdens, which can stunt our potential and ability to serve God and His people. It is for this reason that many people refer to this as simply the year of release. It is a special and significant year where God releases His people from debt and other burdens, which limit our ability to actualize our potential. As a matter of fact, the concept of western bankruptcy laws and removing items from one's name (credit) after seven years is based on the concept of the Shemitah.

It is because the Shemitah is such a critical year for removing debts and burdens, that I believe that the children of Israel were freed from their bondage and debt to Egypt during a Shemitah Year. Why? First, the children of Israel were freed from their debts and bondage to Israel. Also, in that same year Egypt was **overthrown**, which is one of the other meanings and manifestations of the Shemitah Year. This leads us to our discussion of the other side of the Shemitah Year. So far, we have discussed the blessing, freedom, and provision of the Shemitah. Now, we will examine the shaking and overthrowing of nations that occurs during a Shemitah Year.

# A YEAR OF SHAKING

*"The Lord also will roar from Zion, and utter His voice from Jerusalem; The heavens and the earth will shake; but the LORD will be a shelter for His people, and the strength of the children of Israel"* (Joel 3:16)

Earlier we defined the Shemitah Year as a year of releasing others from debt and a year of remission or suspension of (agricultural) labor. It is a year when the land is allowed to rest and in that sense it is the Sabbath of the land, bringing a great blessing to those who observe the Shemitah. However, the Hebrew word translated as "Shemitah" also means to throw down, to overthrow and also refers to a shaking. In this sense the Shemitah Year comes as a year of great shaking. It is a year where foundations are tested and everything that is not built on the Rock solid foundation of God and His Messiah may collapse and suffer substantial loss. Look at what the writer of Hebrews has to say about the shaking that God brings (during a Shemitah):

*"Whose voice then shook the earth; but now He has promised, saying Yet once more I shake not only the earth, but also heaven. Now this, yet once more, indicates the removal of those things that are being shaken, as of things that are made, that the things which cannot be shaken may remain. Therefore, since we are receiving a Kingdom which cannot be shaken, let us have grace, by which we may serve God acceptably with reverence and godly fear. For our God is a consuming fire."* (Hebrews 12:26-29)

# A YEAR WHEN GOD TESTS OUR FOUNDATIONS

*"Whoever comes to Me, and hears My sayings and does them, I will show you whom he is like: He is like a man building a house, who dug deep and laid the foundation on the rock. And when the flood arose, the stream beat vehemently against that house, and could not shake it, for it was founded on the rock."* (Luke 6:47-48)

From the previous passage there are a couple things of importance that we need to discuss. This first idea of great importance is that there is a specific and acceptable way to serve God during a Shemitah Year. There is a way that ensures that one remains on the foundation of the Kingdom, which cannot be shaken. This way shields one from loss and can even attract the blessings of the Kingdom to an individual or nation. This idea we will discuss in much more detail in a later chapter, as it holds the key to what I believe is the most important thing for us to understand if you are living in a nation that may experience the shaking or collapse that is brought about during the Shemitah Year.

The second idea of great importance from the previous Scripture is that God brings shaking to remove those things that are made by man whose origin or source is man and not God. These are things that will shake and fall during a Shemitah. Essentially, anything that is not being built on God's foundation can fall. That means your health, your marriage, your family, your business, your church, your government etc... may be shaken and suffer loss, if it is not on the right foundation. With that said, you can understand that it is also very important to check the foundation of everything you are building and make any necessary corrections.

# THE HISTORICAL EVIDENCE OF THE SHEMITAH

*"That which has been is what will be, that which is done is what will be done, and there is nothing new under the sun. Is there anything of which it may be said see, this is new? It has already*

*been in ancient times before us. There is no remembrance of former things, nor will there be any remembrance of things that are to come by those will come after."* (Ecclesiastes 1:9-11)

For many who have just begun to study the Shemitah and its significance, it may seem as if this is all just some new phenomenon. However, nothing can be further from the truth. As King Solomon explains in the Scripture above, it is not that this is a new occurrence, but rather one we have forgotten. Perhaps we did not realize that this Shemitah phenomenon has been at work every seventh year from the beginning. If that is the case, then there should be a trail of evidence of events that occurred in and around the seventh year throughout history, where we see shakings and individuals and nations experience loss or collapse.

We will now turn our attention to examine some of the Shemitah Years of the past and see there was indeed evidence of shaking, which by the way could come in several forms. On a national level a shaking could be war, or the collapse of a nation, but it could also be a shaking of an economy or a financial recession or depression. So now let's look for some evidence of the Shemitah from the past:

## YEAR        EVENTS

| YEAR | EVENTS |
|------|--------|
| 2007-2008 | Financial Collapse/Global Recession - The Single largest drop in the Stock market in one day. The Dow fell by 777pts. $11 trillion of wealth was lost. |
| 2000- | 9/11 Terrorist attack. On Sept. 17th, 2001 (Elul 29 on God's calendar), the last day for wiping out debts, |

| | |
|---|---|
| 2001 | the market fell by 684 points. This was the largest one day decline in the market prior to that time. |
| 1986-1987 | The Stock Market Crash of 1987, which is ominously referred to as "Black Monday" |
| 1979-1980 | The U.S. entered a deep economic recession; Inflation rose to 13.5% |
| 1972-1973 | January 22, 1973 the Supreme court issues its decision on Roe v Wade on the side of abortion. The price of oil spiked by 200%, which triggered a recession and gas shortages. Israel and Arab nations fought in the Yom Kippur War. |
| 1944-1945 | World War 2 ended and the first atomic bomb was used (on Japan). |
| 1937-1938 | World War 2 Started with the empire of Japan at war with the Republic of China seeking to dominate Asia and the pacific. |
| 1930-1931 | The Great Depression, banks begin to collapse |
| 1860-1861 | Abraham Lincoln was elected as president of the United States on November 6th, 1860. On April 12, 1961 the civil war began. |
| 1811-1812 | The War of 1812 between the United States and the British Empire began June 18, 1812 |
| 1790-1791 | The United States Bill of Rights is ratified. |
| 1776- | The American Revolutionary war; America signed |

| 1777 | the Declaration of Independence. |
|-------|----------------------------------|
| 1769-1770 | On March 5th, 1770 the Boston massacre occurred where British troops killed 5 civilians who were opposed to the heavy tax burden. |

# BY COINCIDENCE OR APPOINTMENT?

*"Then the LORD appointed a set time, saying tomorrow the LORD will do this thing in the land."* (Exodus 9:5)

After looking at the list of major events that greatly impacted the world, hinging on the seventh year, you might be wondering "Is this is just coincidence?" Could it just be just a lucky chance that these things occurred during the Shemitah? However, when you consider the sheer odds of these tremendous events happening in a year that God has also called a year of shaking, you begin to realize that this isn't just some odd chance. We could easily go on examining the Shemitah Years throughout history and you will see that indeed nations have been shaken and many have fallen as a result of events in the seventh years.

This principle and Kingdom decree regarding the seventh year is so significant that you will likely discover that even major biblical events in which there was shaking or a collapse of a nation or nations pivoted on a seventh year. For example, the Flood of Noah's day, the fall of the tower of Babel, the destruction of Sodom and Gomorrah, the famine of Joseph's day, the deliverance of the Children of Israel from Egypt, the establishing of the Davidic kingdom, the fall of Israel to Babylon etc... How many of these events linked to the seventh year?

# BE AWARE OF THE SEVENTH YEAR

*"Speak also to the children of Israel, saying; surely My Sabbaths you shall keep, for it is a sign between Me and you throughout your generations, that you man know that I am the LORD who sanctifies you."* (Exodus 31:13)

The point of referencing to events of the past which likely happened in a Shemitah is not to do an in-depth analysis, but to heighten your awareness of the significance of the seventh year. Why? The seventh year, more than any other year, has more potential to bring about change and transformation. Furthermore, if you understand this, then you can be more like the sons of Issachar who had the skill to discern what to do during divinely appointed times. (1 Chronicles 12:32) By the way, if you would like a more comprehensive analysis of the Shemitah Year, I strongly suggest you read "The Mystery of the Shemitah" by Jonathan Cahn. He has laid a tremendous foundation for understanding the significance of the Shemitah for anyone at any level. This work is to help us to understand what we should do as a result. (1 Chronicles 12:32)

We shall now move on to a more applicable understanding the Shemitah Year. I know and have heard of many people, including church leaders, who don't give much thought to the significance of the seventh year, because they feel like it doesn't matter. Some feel as though there is nothing they can do. Then there are some who just don't see a present day application and use of this information. So the remainder of this book will be dedicated toward the present day application of the Shemitah Year.  If you know of individuals who have already read or heard about the Shemitah and just looking for information on what we should do in a Shemitah Year, the remaining portion of this book will be a great guide for them.

# CHAPTER 3

# WHAT DOES THIS SHEMITAH YEAR MEAN FOR US?

*"But God is the Judge: He puts down one, and exalts another."*
(Psalm 75:7)

This verse is very relevant to our understanding of what this Shemitah Year means to us. It reminds us that God is The Judge and that He puts down one and exalts another. As we discussed earlier, the Shemitah is a word that means to throw down, or overthrow, but it also means to release. As such, it is a year where God demotes one and promotes another, a year where nations and individuals rise and fall. But what does this have to do with the Shemitah Year itself? Why is the Shemitah Year a time when God judges and determines who or what is promoted or demoted?

# THE TIME OF COMPLETION

To understand why the Shemitah Year is also a time of judging, we must first consider when the Shemitah takes place. When? It occurs every seventh year on God's calendar. On Tishrei 1 (on God's calendar), which was at sundown on September 24th, 2014 we entered a seventh year. This Shemitah Year which we are currently in will conclude on Elul 29 (on God's calendar), which will be at sundown on September 13th, 2015. So now that we know the timeline of the current seventh year, let's discuss how or why the seventh year is synonymous with judging. To start, we will go back to the foundation of everything and look at look at the first mention of the word "seven" in scripture and apply the law of first mention to gain a better understanding of the significance of seven.

*"And on the seventh day God ended His work which He had done, and He rested on the seventh day from all His work which He had done."* (Genesis 2:2)

In the previous passage we see the first mention of the word "seventh" in Scripture. It is found at the conclusion and completion of God creating the Heavens and earth and all that is in them. The word translated as seven here is *"shebee"* a word that shares the same Hebrew root as the word translated in this passage as "rested", which is *"Shabath".* This helps paint a picture for us of the word seven having to do with the completion of a task or thing. So from the very first mention of the word *"shebee"* (seven) it is equated with completion. Furthermore, the word translated as "ended" is "kalah" and it refers to the end and completion of a thing.

Now that we understand that seven represents the completion of a thing, we have a better foundation for understanding why the seventh year also represents a year of judging, where God determines promotion and demotion. (Psalm 75:6-7) Why? Only after a task or work is completed can one truly make a quality assessment of their work and determine what needs correction and what needs removal. In this context, we can see that the Shemitah (seventh) year represents a time of analysis after a cycle has been completed. Another way of looking at it is that the Shemitah Year represents a year of pruning. (John 15:1-2)

# WE FORGOT GOD IS A JUDGE

*"For exaltation comes neither from the east nor from the west nor from the south. But God is the Judge: He puts down one, and exalts another."* (Psalm 75:6-7)

Perhaps not in your circle, but it is clear that many, even in the church have forgotten that God is not just a judge, but "The Judge." Consider this analogy... In the United States, we have a constitution that is the sole governing agent for the land. Others are authorized to weigh actions against this document. However, no one is authorized to change the standards in this course of action. In the same regard, God is the one who has the supreme authority for His creation. He has determined the standard by which his create in judged. As a matter of fact, the evidence that God is The Judge becomes more apparent when you look more closely at the word translated "God." The Hebrew word often translated as God is *"Elohim"* (אלהים) and it refers to God as a Ruler or Judge Who alone has the authority to evaluate and assess His creation.

Now that we understand that a seventh year, or Shemitah Year, represents a cycle of completion and that The Judge is making His assessment and evaluation for what needs pruning and what needs promoting, you may be wondering what lies ahead. Since we have determined that a Shemitah Year also represents a year of shaking, where God tests foundations, we have to consider our own foundation and whether we are on the Rock, which cannot be shaken. (Hebrews 12:28) Will we see collapse in our nation's economy or government? Where will we see pruning or promotion? What should we expect during this Shemitah Year?

# ANALYZING THE PATTERNS OF RECENT SHEMITAH YEARS

As we try to determine what is ahead for the nations of the world during this current Shemitah Year, we must first look at the past and analyze any patterns that may help us predict what may lie ahead. With that being stated let's review events which occurred during the past two seven year cycles.

On September 29, 2008, and September 17, 2001 were the same days on the biblical calendar. Both dates happened to fall on Elul 29, exactly 7 years apart. These were the last day of the Shemitah Year and the final day for shaking and canceling debts. On September 29, 2008, the Dow Jones fell by 777 points. That was indeed an astounding 7% drop. As of today, this is the largest one day drop in the history of the market. It has been estimated that just in the U.S. alone, families lost $11 trillion in wealth. Some political and economic leaders believed that we actually came within a few hours of a global economic meltdown. It was in fact this belief which led to the economic stimulus package or bailout in the amount of $700 billion. According to many economists today, the world has never truly recovered from this economic crisis.

The previous Shemitah Year, overlapped the years of 2000 and 2001. On September 11, 2001 came the greatest terrorist attack on U.S. soil, in which the Twin Towers of the World Trade Center "collapsed" and the U.S. Pentagon was damaged. In all, over 3000 lives were lost on that day leading to a war with Afghanistan and a war with Iraq. That's not all. Because of the terror attack on 9/11 the markets closed and when they reopened on September 17, 2001, Elul 29, the Dow Jones fell by 684 points. Prior to 2008, this date was largest one day drop in the market in our nation's history. So what can we gain from examining the last two Shemitah Years? Is there some kind of pattern emerging that you can see? If this current Shemitah follows the pattern of the last two, what might we see? Well, from the past two Shemitahs we saw terror attacks, which lead to a long war on terror. Consequently, we will look to see if there is any information current with this seventh year, which would support the potential or possibility of more war.

By analyzing the last two cycles, we see commonalities and a potential pattern emerging, We see terror attacks, war, and financial calamity. Not only did we see a market crash in both 2001 and 2008, but each crash was greater than any crash prior to it. So, is it possible that we could see an even greater financial crash in 2015 than we seen in 2008? We'll take a look to see if there is any current info that supports the potential of a greater financial collapse than we saw in 2008.

# HOW REAL IS THE THREAT OF WAR DURING THIS SHEMITAH YEAR?

When looking for any current information that would support the potential of a new large-scale war, we don't have to look too deeply. In 2014, we saw the rise of a terror group called ISIS, whose goal, according to many experts, is to establish a caliphate. It is because of such ambitious goals and ideals possessed by its leaders and followers alike, that many consider ISIS to be a much greater threat than Al-Qaeda.

However, don't be mistaken in thinking that ISIS is the only real potential threat for a new large-scale war. North of the Middle

East you can hear the saber rattling of Russia, whose current leader has long had the ambition of seeing the reunification of the former Soviet Union. In 2014 we saw evidence of Russia's desire when it invaded Ukraine, which was once part of the Soviet Union. In spite of sanctions and strong disapproval from the west, Russia marched ahead and invaded a nation that is supposed to be under the protection of the United Nations. So far all we have seen from the west and the United States are sanctions and the proposal of more sanctions, which will continue to increase the tension between Russia and the west.

Is there a possibility of war with Russia on a global scale during this Shemitah Year? You do the math, but then also remember that many major wars have begun or ended during a Shemitah Year. In conclusion of our analysis of a Shemitah war, I suggest, as Yeshua instructed us, that you watch and pray. (Luke 21:36)

# HOW GREAT IS THE THREAT OF A FINANCIAL AND ECONOMIC COLLAPSE DURING THIS SHEMITAH YEAR?

Knowing that the Shemitah is also a year that has ominously affected the financial markets and economies of the world in years past, makes it hard to not at least consider the possibilities of financial catastrophe during this current Shemitah. Also considering that the last two Shemitah Years brought colossal drops in the in the financial markets and global economy, it would be foolish to not at least make inquiries about the matter.

Is there any current news or information which could mean financial ruin for individuals and nations in this year? Well let's start with something that is probably old news to most. It is now estimated that the total U.S. debt is now over $18 trillion! That comes out to about $56,000 in debt per U.S. citizen (just those living in America). If you pay taxes, it means $154,128 of debt per tax payer. This may not seem significant to you in this digital age in which we live, but many economists believe that it is impossible for the U.S. to repay such a colossal debt. That means at some point the U.S. will default on its debt.

In other current economic news, the IMF (or International Monetary Fund) and G7 (nations with the top seven economies) continue to push forward the idea of replacing the dollar as the world reserve currency and supplanting it with what is being called an SDR (special drawing right). According to many economists, this would put the U.S. on the fastest path to hyperinflation, quicker than all other economic factors. Could the death of the dollar as the world reserve currency happen this year? The Business Insider reported on October 8, 2014, within two weeks after this current Shemitah Year began that for the first time in recent history China surpassed the U.S. as the world's number one economy. By the way, this is not just coincidence. Why was this date significant? It was the eve of the Feast of Tabernacles and a day on which a blood moon occupied the skies. Is this a sign or omen for the United States? Watch and pray.

# SIGNS FROM HEAVEN DURING THIS SHEMITAH

Earlier we discussed the significance of signs in the heavens during divinely appointed seasons. We explained that according to Scripture (Genesis 1:14) when the cosmic lights (like the sun, moon, stars, comets etc...) are aligned and interact in certain ways, that it is a signal or warning to us from God. Well it just so happens that shortly after this current Shemitah Year began (2014-2015), we saw a blood moon at the start of the festival of Tabernacles (October 8th, 2014). Moreover, according to NASA, we will see two more blood moons and two solar eclipses during this Shemitah Year. Here are the dates below on both the western calendar and God's calendar for the blood moons and solar eclipses of this current Shemitah Year:

| EVENT CALENDAR | WESTERN CALENDAR | GOD'S CALENDAR |
| --- | --- | --- |
| Lunar Eclipse (Blood Moon) | October 8th, 2014 | Tishrei 14 5775 |
| Solar Eclipse | March 20th, 2015 | Adar 29 5775 |
| Lunar Eclipse (Blood Moon) | April 4th, 2015 | Nissan 15 5775 |

| Solar Ecliplse | September 13<sup>th</sup>, 2015 | Elul 29 5775 |
| --- | --- | --- |
|  |  |  |

What do these signs mean?  What is significant about a blood moon or solar eclipse during *moedim* or divinely appointed times?  According to some of the great sages of times past, a blood moon during *moedim* was viewed as a warning sign of impending judgment or war for the nation of Israel. Furthermore, a solar eclipse was viewed as a sign of judgment or war for the nations of the world.

Could there be any merit to this?  Well, consider the following and you be the judge:  On Passover in 2014 (April 14<sup>th</sup>, 2014), there was a lunar eclipse or blood moon.  Just a few months later on July 8<sup>th</sup>, Israel and Hamas were at war over the Gaza strip. Coincidence?  Probably not.  Let's move on to see if there have been any occurrences of solar eclipses during a divinely appointed season, which appeared as sign of judgment.  On Elul 29 (or September 23<sup>rd</sup>), 1987 at the end of a Shemitah Year there was also a solar eclipse.  A month later on October 19<sup>th</sup>, the markets took a huge dive, a day that has been ominously referred to since as "Black Monday."

What is ahead for the nations of the world during this Shemitah Year?  Just as in 1987 there will be another solar eclipse on Elul 29.  Could there be another Black Monday event?  If we follow the pattern of the last two Shemitah Years, we should expect another huge drop in the markets globally without Divine intervention.  Many people who are well aware of the threats faced by our world have begun to prepare for the worst.  As a matter of fact, in the last few years the "prepping industry" has become a multi-billion dollar industry. It is just as Yeshua said, *"And there will be signs in the sun, in the moon, and in the stars; and on the earth distress of nations, with perplexity, the sea and the waves roaring; mens hearts failing them from fear and the expectation of those things which are coming on the earth, for the powers of the heavens will be shaken."* (Luke 21:25-26)

In light of these things, what should we do? How are we to respond to these things? Should we buy gold and silver? Should we store up food and ammo? Should we move out to the country and away from urban areas? What is the answer from Heaven? In the next chapter we will examine the Scriptures to see if we can understand what God expects of us, particularly during a Shemitah Year.

# CHAPTER 4

# WHAT DOES GOD DESIRE FROM US DURING A SHEMITAH YEAR?

*"For the LORD gives wisdom; from His mouth come knowledge and understanding; He stores up sound wisdom for the upright; He is a shield to those who walk uprightly."* (Proverbs 2:6-7)

Let me first say that I am not going to advise you against preparing for the worst. In my humble opinion storing food, water, herbal medicines and monetary assets such as gold and silver is a wise idea. Why? Because even if things continue as they have and society remains (somewhat) stable, you still possess things will maintain their value to you. On the other hand to not have these things in any state of emergency could bring about a struggle for the survival for you and your loved ones. Even King Solomon encouraged us to glean from the wisdom of the ants which stores food for winter during the summer. (Proverbs 30:25) However, having said that prepping in the natural is a good idea, I do not believe that it should be your top priority. Why? Ultimately this year of shaking is from God the judge of all the earth. If He has decreed that calamity must come or that blessing must come, what can we do to oppose His will? Sure you can prepare and load up on food and ammo, but here's what the Scripture says about our efforts;

*"Unless the LORD guards the city the watchman stays awake in vain."* (Psalm 127:1)

In the long run, it doesn't matter how much we prepare in the natural if we don't do what is spiritually required for our protection and deliverance from evil.

In the scripture from Proverbs listed above, we are reminded that wisdom (which is the ability to skillfully apply knowledge) comes from God. It is He who gives understanding of what to do and what steps we need to take at various times in life. Furthermore, it is He who shields those who walk uprightly from perilous times. If there are rocky times ahead for the nations, then our first priority should be to "seek first the Kingdom of God, and all of His righteousness and all of the things you need for life shall be added to you." (Matthew 6:33)

# ALIGN YOURSELF WITH THE KINGDOM

By we aligning ourselves with God's (Kingdom) instructions, pursuing opportunities to serve others in love, being a blessing, God will not only shield us from calamity, but He will supply us with what we need. Now let's take a closer look at what the LORD instructs us to do during a Shemitah Year.

For those who have already read or heard information about the seventh year, this section will help you understand what to do. If there is socioeconomic calamity for the world in the days ahead, the information we are about to now share will be more valuable than any amount of gold, silver, food or water storage you can stockpile. Before we get into the details I want to remind you what the Scripture says the mindset of Kingdom citizens should be.

*"Therefore I say to you, do not worry about your life, what you will eat or what you will drink; nor about your body, what you will put on. Is not life more than food and the body more than clothing?*

*Look at the birds of the air, for they neither sow nor reap nor gather into barns; yet your heavenly Father feeds them. Are you not of more value than they? Which of you by worrying can add one cubit to his stature? So why do you worry about clothing? Consider the lilies of the field, how they grow: they neither toil nor spin; and yet I say to you that even Solomon in all his glory was not arrayed like one of these. Now if God so clothes the grass of the field, which today is and tomorrow is thrown in to the oven, will He not much more clothe you, O you of little faith? Therefore do now worry, saying, what shall we eat? Or what shall we drink? Or what shall we wear? For after all these things the Gentiles seek. For your Heavenly Father knows that you need all these things. But seek first the Kingdom of God and His righteousness, and all these things shall be added to you. Therefore do not worry about tomorrow, for tomorrow will worry about its own things. Sufficient for the day is its own trouble."* (Matthew 6:25-34)

# THE YEAR OF RELEASE

*"At the end of every seven years you shall grant a release of debts."*
(Deuteronomy 15:1)

The year of release is a popular phrase or expression often heard in many charismatic churches at the beginning of the year. Usually when the phrase is heard it is in the context of a pastor or minister declaring that a new year will bring a release of God's blessings on an individual or congregation. In this Scripture we also see God speaking of a release as well, but the objective and beneficiary of this release spoken of in Deuteronomy seems to be directed towards others. This is in contrast to how this phrase is often used or heard in some congregations. Usually when people hear of the LORD'S release, they are viewed as being on the receiving end of this release (of blessings). However, in Deuteronomy 15:1, God instructs His people to **grant** a release of debts to others in the Shemitah Year.

What exactly does God mean by "you shall grant a release of debts?" It is imperative that you understand that this is the first thing God instructs us to do during the seventh year. Remember "first" is an indicator of priority, which means that granting a release of debts is more important than storing up food, water and gold. Therefore, you may want to pay close attention to an explanation on how to grant a release of debts.

# A YEAR TO RELIEVE PRESSURE AND STRESS

The Hebrew word often translated as debt is *"neshiy"* and it does refer to something owed, and often with interest. Usually this word is used in the context of money owed to someone else. However, that is not the only correct context of the word *"neshiy"* (debt).

The Hebrew pictograph of the word makes it even easier to understand its true meaning and significance. The word *neshiy* is from two Hebrew root letters. The *nun* (נ) which is a picture of a seed and represents multiplication or continuance and *shin* (שׁ) which is a picture of teeth and represents the idea of consuming or pressure. Combined, these create a pictograph of *neshiy* as a continuous pressure. That means that *neshiy* in its correct context is not about monetary debt as much as it is about things that continuously keep pressure on people. So now let us insert this understanding in Deuteronomy 15:1 and see if there is difference: *"At the end of every seven years you shall grant a release from continuous pressure."*

Do you see the difference? In the Shemitah Year, God wants you to be especially intentional about freeing people from things that cause them to feel pressured and overly burdened. Since pressure causes stress, which can lead to a multitude of health issues, we can say that in a Shemitah Year we are to seek to eliminate stress in people's lives due to burdens they may be under. But wait...does the idea of being commissioned to relieve people of their burdens sound at all familiar? If so, it may be because you have heard or read the following verse:

*"Come to Me, all you who labor and are heavy laden, and I will give you rest. Take My yoke upon you and learn from Me, for I am gentle and lowly in heart, and you will find rest for your souls. For My yoke is easy and My burden is light."* (Matthew 11:28-30)

Although I am not sure, I wouldn't at all be surprised if Yeshua made the previous statement during a Shemitah Year. I mean if you had only one in seven years to make that declaration, clearly the most likely year for it is the seventh year, which is the year of releasing people from continuous pressure. In this Scripture we see Yeshua declaring that He had come for those who were under continuous pressures and burdens from life.

# RECEIVE GOD'S ANOINTING TO RELEASE OTHERS

*"For You have broken the yoke of his burden and the staff of his shoulder, the rod of his oppressor, as in the day of Midian."* (Isaiah 9:4)

If you have read or studied the Scriptures you may be aware that the LORD has a history of anointing people to do great and mighty things. There is a long list of individuals who have done marvelous things while under the anointing. For example, it was because he was anointed that Samson, slew the lion with his bare hands and a thousand Philistines at one time with the jaw bone of a donkey (Judges 14:6; 15:14-15). It was because of the anointing that David slew the giant Goliath (1Samuel 16:13; 17:45-50).

So what does it mean to be anointed? Perhaps an even more relevant question is, what does the anointing have to do with the Shemitah Year? The Hebrew word translated as anointed is *"mashach"* and on the surface it means to consecrate someone to a particular task by smearing them with oil. Usually it was a king or priest who was anointed. As a matter of fact, the word Messiah, which is *"moshiach"* is related to the word for anointed *"mashach."* However, there were other things which were also anointed, for example, the furniture of the Tabernacle was also anointed. Furthermore, after someone or something was anointed, it became *qadosh* (holy) and was connected directly to the Spirit of God to carry out its function.

So in the proper or correct context, the purpose of the anointing is to consecrate and spiritually empower someone to carry out God's purpose. Take a look at the following Scripture and we will begin to see how this anointing is especially important to the task of liberating people from pressures and burdens.

# ANOINTED TO REMOVE BURDENS

*"It shall come to pass in that day that his burden will be taken away from your shoulder, and his yoke from your neck, and the yoke will be destroyed because of the anointing oil."* (Isaiah 10:27)

Now do you see the importance of the anointing during a Shemitah Year? It is the anointing of God that empowers us to remove burdens from someone's shoulder and to destroy yokes (of bondage). I'm sure since you're human or normal, you would ask, "How in the natural can I release people from debt and burdens on my own?" That's just it, you don't have to do it own your own. If you are willing and obedient, God will anoint you for such a task. He will authorize and empower you to do what cannot be done without His aid. Do you remember God's conversation with Moses when He asked him to go free the children of Israel.

*"Now therefore, behold, the cry of the children of Israel has come to Me, and I have also seen the oppression with which the Egyptians oppress them. Come now, therefore and I will send you to Pharaoh that you may bring My people, the Children of Israel, out of Egypt. But Moses said to God, who am I that I should go to Pharaoh, and that I should bring the Children of Israel out of Egypt? So He said, I will certainly be with you. And this shall be a sign to you that I have sent you: When you have brought the people out of Egypt, you shall serve God on this mountain."* (Exodus 3:9-12)

# A SPECIAL YEAR FOR ANOINTING

As I said before, I wouldn't be at all surprised if Moses was also called to deliver the children of Israel from Egypt during a Shemitah Year. The significance of the year of release as a year where God brings great deliverance from burdens and oppression cannot be understated. If God only had one in seven years, that He would remove burdens and destroy yokes, it is of little doubt that year would be the seventh year, "The Year of Release." God's people should be greatly encouraged to know that we are in a year when God's yoke destroying, burden removing anointing is abundantly available to empower us to set people free and even save them from destruction.

To be sure the seventh year is a special year for uncommon anointing. Remember the Shemitah Year is a year of judgment for individuals and nations who have gone away from God's foundation. It is a year when many will experience shaking, or collapse. Such a collapse could come in the form of a financial or economic downfall or even war.

If you have seen or experienced the results of economic collapse or war, you probably know all too well that these types of events cause people to live under an unusual amount of continuous pressure and stress. This kind of pressure has often led to the collapse of morals and values. It can cause a collapse in families and communities as people become desperate and willing to do all kinds of ungodly acts to try and ensure their own survival.

There is good news! In anticipation of the coming shaking, not only is God warning us, but He is calling for and preparing a people who will grant a release of *"nishiy"* (continuous pressure) that many will face. Later we will look even more closely at the idea of releasing others from debts and burdens. Right now, it was important to just introduce the concept and lay a foundation to build on this idea. Now let's identify another important expectation God has for us during a Shemitah Year.

# IS THERE ANOTHER WAY?

I truly thank God for His plan to deliver those who are in trouble and under pressure. However, is there a way to avoid God's judgment altogether? Is it possible to attract God's blessing and favor even if judgment and calamity has already been decreed for an individual or nation? In the last two Shemitah Years (2001 & 2008) we saw terror attacks and financial collapse which left many impoverished and over-burdened. Yet, in spite of those events America as a nation has still decided to stray further from God and His plan for our lives and our nation.

In the natural, there is no reason for America to expect that the shaking brought about by this current Shemitah Year will not be considerably greater than the last two. According to the Scripture, when God desires to turn a nation from its ways, He allows terror and greater catastrophic events to occur until a nation either repents or is no more (Leviticus 26:14-39). How can we turn God's judgment from our nation(s)? Is there a way out?

Yes, there is a way out. It is possible to turn God's wrath. Surprisingly the answer is simple. If we want to turn God's judgment, then we must turn. In the Scripture, this idea of turning is called repentance. In the next section of the book we will take a closer look at what it really means to repent, and why or how is it that our repentance can turn God's judgment and attract His favor.

# CHAPTER 5

# THE POWER OF TRUE REPENTANCE

*"The instant I speak concerning a nation and concerning a kingdom, to pluck up, to pull down, and to destroy it, if that nation against whom I have spoken turns from its evil, I will relent of the disaster that I thought to bring upon it."* (Jeremiah 18:7-8)

The idea and concept of repentance is one of the most important and powerful concepts found in Scripture. True repentance is one of the ways we make amends for our imperfection. Where there is true repentance, the atmosphere is set for the most miraculous of events to occur. It is my opinion and belief along with many others, that true repentance is America's *only* hope for not only returning to her former glory, but the only hope she has for becoming a greater nation, one with whom God is well pleased. So if America doesn't want to see greater terror attacks or a greater financial collapse than seen in 2001 and 2008, then America *must* repent.

But what does it mean to truly repent? Is it just the act of an individual or nation expressing sorrow for offending God? Is repentance when an individual prays and asks God for forgiveness for offenses or disobedience? No! In and of themselves those things are not repentance. However, they can be viewed as things that accompany true repentance.

So what is repentance and how do we attain it? The Hebrew word translated as repentance is *"teshuvah"* from the root word *"shuv"*, which means to return. This word *"shuv"* is first found in Scripture in Genesis 3:19 when God tells man that he came from the dust and that he shall **_return_** to the dust. The second time this word is used is in Genesis 8:13 after the great flood, when

Scripture records that the waters **_returned_** to their place.  So according to the Hebraic principles of hermeneutics and the law of first mention, we can conclude that in order to truly repent or *"teshuvah"* we must return to our proper place and position.  This also means regardless of what we do in an effort to repent, if we do not somehow return to our place with God, then we have not truly repented.

# THE PLACE OF REPENTANCE

Throughout the Scripture, God's people have often sought repentance during times of judgment or calamity.  Often we see what appears to be a cycle of sorts, where God's people are delivered from oppression, then they prosper, which is followed by a time of drifting away from their place with God, which is followed by a time of being given over to their enemies, which is followed by a time of repentance, which is again followed by God's deliverance.  To say that repentance has played a vital role in the lives of God's people is a serious understatement.

Unfortunately, there are those who mistakenly believe that God's judgments and/or decision to be passive in allowing calamity to come upon His people is because He is intent on destroying us.  This could not be further from the truth.  As a matter of fact, the Scripture records for us exactly how God feels when people face destruction:

*"Say to them:  As I live, says the LORD God, I have no pleasure in the death of the wicked, but that the wicked **turn** from his way and live.  **Turn, turn** from your evil ways!  For why should you die, O house of Israel?"* (Ezekiel 33:11 *emphasis added).

Three times in this Scripture, God emphatically states the purpose of allowing calamity to come upon His people. It is not because He takes pleasure in destroying those who act wickedly, but because He wants them to turn from their evil ways.

As you probably guessed, the word translated as "turn" in the previous Scripture is *"shuv"*, the root word for *teshuvah* and returning to our place with God. So again it is confirmed here that God's purpose in allowing catastrophe is to encourage man to leave his path of evil and return to his place with God. So we must understand that repentance is not a prayer, as much as it is a place. Repentance is both returning to our place in God *and* allowing God to return to His place within and among us. In the next chapter we will take a closer look at the role of prayer in repentance.

# WHEN IS THE TIME OF REPENTANCE?

*"When I shut up heaven and there is no rain, or command the locusts to devour the land, or send pestilence among My people, if My people who are called by My name will humble themselves, and pray and seek My face, and turn from their wicked ways, then I will hear from heaven, and will forgive their sin and heal their land."* (2 Chronicles 7:14)

Without out a doubt this Scripture is the most well-known and quoted Scripture for a nation in need of repentance. Not only does it explain when a nation should repent, but it also lists the process for achieving true repentance and turning God's judgment into God's favor. In examining this Scripture we will first look at when repentance is required and then we will examine the process and prerequisites of true *teshuvah.*

# WHAT ARE THE SIGNS REPENTANCE IS NECESSARY?

How can a nation know when they should repent?  What are the signs that such action is required?  Since true repentance *(teshuvah)* is defined as returning to your place with God, one can first diagnose the need for repentance by analyzing their place with God.  If a nation removes God from His place in their midst or in their hearts, then it is time to repent.  If a nation begins to remove God's influence and instructions from their governing laws, then it is time to *teshuvah.*  If a nation and its people begin to set up idols in their heart and no longer adhere to God's teaching or instructions, it is time to repent.

# THE SIGN OF RAIN

After the initial diagnosis and acknowledgment that a nation has left its place with God and yet there is no attempt to return, consequences will follow.  One of the first consequences of a nation not repenting is that God will shut up the heavens and hold back the rain.  This rain does not necessarily refer to physical precipitation, although it could.  In Scripture rain is also used as a metaphor to represent the thing that causes the earth to yield her produce.  Look at what God says about the rains causing the earth to produce:

*"For as the rain comes down, and the snow from heaven, and do not return there, but water the earth. And make it bring forth and bud, that it may give seed to the sower and bread to the eater..."* (Isaiah 55:10)

From this context, we can understand that a lack of rain means a lack of produce and productivity in a nation's economy. It means that a nation's economy is slowed, and its GDP is decreased. It means that a nation transitions from having predominately producers to having predominately consumers.

For those in a nation who remain in their proper place with God, they quickly realize the nations need to return (repent). They become like the prophets of ancient Israel, who warned the nation's people and its government that they must *teshuvah* or things will get worse. Unfortunately, these prophets were usually persecuted, thrown in jail, or worse. Why? The people and its government who had left their place with God had become insensitive and blinded to the warning signs. They began to take for granted the One who had sustained their nation. They were too busy enjoying the life of a being a consumer to realize that without producing, things would come to a halt. Does this sound familiar? Have you noticed a division in the United States between those who say we are in trouble, versus those who say things are fine, if not better than before?

Do not be deceived, the economy will not fix itself without rain from Heaven. Moreover, the heavens will not yield sufficient rain if the country does not return to its place with God as its Leader and Lawgiver. No bailout or economic stimulus package will repair the situation. No vote or change in political leadership will repair the economy if the nation is not lead to true repentance.

# THE SIGN OF THE LOCUST

The second sign of a nation in need of repentance is when the locust began to devour the land. This sign is probably challenging to grasp for most people. To understand this metaphor we need to understand the role of the locust as identified in Scripture. The word translated as locust is *"chagab"* and it is a word that is often translated in the Scriptures as "grasshopper." Interestingly, according to Leviticus 11:22, the grasshopper (locust) is listed among the foods, which are considered kosher or ceremonially clean to eat.

The first thing you should understand about the locust is that it was edible and considered as something which can be consumed. This makes it a bit challenging to understand the significance of the idea of the locust devouring the land. How can we make sense of something which can be consumed, consuming the land? What would the locust consume? What was their food?

The diet of the locust is one of plants and the produce of the land itself. That means when the locust devour the produce of the land, then there is a shortage or a lack of produce to store up for the future. In this context then we can see that the locust problem represents the idea of a nation consuming tomorrow's produce today. As result of a nation not having enough for tomorrow, it begins to borrow and accumulate massive amounts of debt to sustain itself. A nation under the curse of the locust is doomed to be a debtor nation. It becomes a nation where everything seems to be financed and very little is gained without debt.

What is the sign of the locusts? It is the inability of an individual or nation to save for tomorrow. It represents a destructive habit of consuming all of its produce and resources today without considering that winter is coming. So let me ask again. Does this sound at all familiar? Have you heard disputes between those who say we are spending and consuming too much versus those who say we need to spend more?

As stated before, this is not a problem that can be fixed by a vote or change in political leadership. The locust cannot be voted away. The locust problem will not even be eliminated if a nation begins to significantly increase its productivity. An increase in productivity or produce will simply result in an increase in locusts. Do not be deceived, the locust will only return to their place when a nation returns to its place.

# THE SIGN OF PESTILENCE

The last sign of a nation which needs to *teshuvah* is the sign of pestilence. This sign is probably the most peculiar of all. To understand this sign we will need to look beneath the surface and examine the pictograph of the word translated as pestilence.

The word pestilence is the Hebrew word *"deber"* which refers to disease or various maladies which result in dysfunction and death. Interestingly, this word *deber* is from the root word *dabar* which means "spoken word" or "to communicate with." In this context, that can be viewed as God's attempt to communicate with a nation who has traveled so far from God they cannot hear His voice. It is God's desperate attempt to help a nation hear His call to return. When a nation will not hear God's spoken word *"dabar"* He sends pestilence "deber" in hopes of reaching them through another form of communication.

Now we'll take a look at the pictograph of the word translated pestilence and see if we can gain a deeper connection or understanding. The word pestilence, *"deber"* is formed from the letters *dalet* (ד) which is a picture of an open door, a *bet* (ב) which is a picture of a house or household, and a *resh* (ר) which is a picture of a leader or chief ruler. Together *deber* creates a pictograph of the door of the house being opened by the leadership.

What does this mean you ask? Well, if you think in terms of function, a door's function is to keep on the outside things which may bring harm and destruction to the inside. It is generally the job of the head of a house to guard the door of the house and keep danger out. This danger could be in the form of diseases or even enemies being allowed into the household.

Does this sound familiar? Have you heard discussion of the borders or doors of the nation being not only unguarded, but opened for enemies of the nation to enter? This is the curse of pestilence; and just like the other signs, this cannot be fixed with a vote. Let me just say, it doesn't matter if the Republicans, Democrats or even Independents are in office. If the nation is not led in *teshuvah*, then the doors will remain open and pestilence will increase.

By the way, do you think it was merely coincidence that the first known case of Ebola was diagnosed in the United States on September 30th, 2014, just several days after the commencement of the current Shemitah Year? I think you know better than to believe it was just coincidence. I believe that God was allowing us to see that the door is opened for the sign or curse of pestilence. He is giving us the opportunity to close the door(s) through *teshuvah* in order to prevent a widespread outbreak of disease (deber).

After realizing that the signs of God's call to repentance are clearly evident in our nation, it is time that we get more specific on what true *teshuvah* looks like. What does it look like when an individual or nation truly returns to their place with God? For the rest of this chapter we will examine each step in the process of true repentance, beginning with what it means to humble oneself.

# IF MY PEOPLE WILL HUMBLE THEMSELVES

*"...if My people who are called by My name will humble themselves..."* (2 Chronicles 7:14)

According to the Scripture, after a person has recognized the signs and the need to *teshuvah*, the first step is to humble oneself. The word translated as humble here is the word *"kana"* and it means "to lower oneself" and "to subject oneself to the leadership and guidance of another." To put it another way *"kana"* means submission. As a matter of fact, this is the Hebrew word which describes how a wife is to submit to her husband's leadership.

In the process of repentance, the call to humble oneself is directed to an individual or nation who determine their own ways and believes its ways are better than God's. They act and speak as if God's teachings or instructions are old-fashioned and are no longer relevant to the times in which they live. The need for humility or *kana* is evident in a nation which seeks to remove God's influence from the laws or their nation.

While the idea of humbling oneself may be listed first in the process of *teshuvah*, it is probably the most challenging, especially for a nation that thinks its ways are better than God's. For an individual or nation to truly humble themselves, they must not only submit to, but also acknowledge the One to whom they are submitting. Most importantly, they must follow God's instructions and principles regardless of what ideas are currently trending.

# AND SEEK MY FACE

*"...and pray, seek my face..."* (2 Chronicles 7:14)

The next step in the process of *teshuvah* is to pray, but we will wait until the next chapter to discuss the prayer of *teshuvah* and the prayer of the Shemitah Year. Right now we will examine what it means to seek God's face.

What does it mean to seek the face of God? Often when you hear someone state they are seeking God's face, they are referring to engaging in certain activities, which are deemed to make one more spiritual or holy. Such activities include attending church services, studying God's Word, praying, and fasting. However, is that the meaning of seeking God's face? Is there a Scripture which helps us understand how one can hope to see God's face? There certainly is! To discover this formula for seeking the face of God we need look no further than the writings of someone who God Himself called, a man after His Own heart. Take a look at the Scripture below to see David explain how he would seek the face of God.

*"As for me, I will see Your face in righteousness; I shall be satisfied when I awake in Your likeness."* (Psalm 17:15)

After reading the inspired words of David, a man after God's own heart, we can conclude that (seeking) righteousness is what would enable him to see the face of God. Now before we go any further it is important that you understand that we are not saying your righteousness is what gets you into Heaven. Seeking the face of God is a metaphor that refers to two very important things. The first aspect of seeking the face of God, refers to gaining proximity or nearness to God. It means to draw near and experience a very present closeness with God. Interestingly, the Hebrew word for drawing near to God, which is *"korban,"* is also the word that means to bring God an offering.

In spite of what your understanding or experience may be in relation to bringing offerings to God, when you truly understand the significance and purpose of offerings you will appreciate why God describes one who brings an offering (korban) as one who has drawn close to Him.

## CLOSE ENOUGH TO SEE HIS INTENTIONS

This second aspect of seeking God's face, means being close enough to God to know certain details that one would only know if one in fact, had a measurable encounter with God. To understand this better, we have to think about the function of one's face and not the form of one's face. In other words, when

God call us to seek His face, He is not admonishing us to be able to describe what he looks like. What is the function of a face? A person's face has a couple important functions; the first is that it reveals their feelings. If a person is happy or angry you can see it on the expression of their face.

The second function of one's face is related to the first. In addition to a person's face revealing their feelings, a person's face also reveals their intentions or purpose. In this sense, to seek God's face means to seek to know and align one's self with His purpose. In the context of 2 Chronicles 7:14, this makes a lot more sense, when you understand what is required for genuine *teshuvah*.

First, we must humble ourselves, which means that we are ready and agree to submit to God's will and purpose, then we are instructed to (pray and) seek His face, which means to seek to understand His will and purpose. From this we can glean that genuine *teshuvah* is evident when an individual or nation first humbles themselves to follow God's leading and actively seek to align their lives with God's will and purpose. Put another way, this also means that if a person is not obeying the known will of God for their lives (in every area) and seeking His purpose that they have not truly repented.

Now that we've addressed what it means to seek the face of God, we will now turn our focus to understanding what David said he would do to seek God's face.

# SEEING HIS FACE THROUGH RIGHTEOUSNESS

*"As for me, I will see Your face in righteousness..."* (Psalm 17:15)

According to David, seeing the face of God was somehow connected to (seeking His) righteousness. What does it mean to seek God through righteousness? Does that mean as long as we believe in Yeshua as Savior we have His righteousness? Where should a person search to find God? Is He found in church or some secluded place away from the chaos of our cities and communities?

In order to understand what it means to seek God in righteousness, we will need to define righteousness from a Kingdom perspective. For many of you the true idea of righteousness, may be a complete redefining of the concept as you previously understood it. So, before we delve into the subject, I want to encourage you to not be afraid to embrace the idea of adding to or cultivating your Kingdom vocabulary.

While in this particular book we will not do an intimate analysis and dissection of the word translated as righteousness, we will do a general overview of the subject. Should you be interested in a more detailed and comprehensive view of righteousness I would encourage you to read (study) "<u>Kingdom Treasury Volume 1</u>." Now let us begin our overview of righteousness.

# UNDERSTANDING RIGHTEOUSNESS

The traditional and contemporary idea of righteousness in Christianity is that it means right standing with God, and that it's a position that one receives strictly because of one's belief in Yeshua. Based on this definition, it is usually deemed that one is righteous because one believes, and not because of what one does. The problem with this definition of righteousness is that it is not a complete or accurate interpretation of the Hebrew word translated as righteousness, which is "*tzedakah*" (צְדָקָה). Contrary to the predominant Christian understanding of righteousness, *tzedakah* (pronounced *se-da-kah)* has everything to do with works. In fact, even though it may sound taboo according to some denominations, *tzedakah* (i.e. righteousness) is about your **GOOD WORKS!**

Righteousness is actually something you *work!* Please do not confuse righteousness with justification. It is justification that we have received by grace, which has nothing to do with good works, but only God's goodness. (Romans 4:25; 5:16)

Furthermore, as we make this important distinction between righteousness *(tzedakah)* and justification *(tzedak)*, it is important that we understand that we are not teaching or endorsing a salvation that is based on works. It is only the Messiah who has delivered and freed us from the guilt and penalty of our sins. Solely as a result of God's grace and what He alone has done, having shouldered the consequence of our sin, we are innocent of sin through Him. However, just being innocent of any wrong doing (sin), does not mean we do good. This is the difference between being justified and being righteous. Being justified means we have been judged as blameless, but being righteous implies that we do good things.

# RIGHTEOUSNESS IS CHARITY AND GENOROSITY

How can the word *tzedakah* mean both charity (i.e. generosity) and justice? Although the word *tzedakah* is more accurately translated as charity, it comes from the Hebrew root word "*tzedek*", which means justice. This is what makes it such a strange word, how can something be justice and charity at the same time? If I owe you something it is not charity when I give it to you, it is justice. Conversely, if I give you something that I did not owe you out of the desire of my heart to be kind and generous, then it is not justice--it is charity (or generosity).

This gets even more interesting when you look closely at the meaning of the words, charity and justice. The word "charity," is from the Latin word *"caritas,"* and means a generous donation or gift given out of love and kindness to help the poor, the sick, and others in need. Charity can involve giving money, food, water, clothes, time and energy (volunteering) or other resources to help out with a particular need.

On the other hand, the word justice means to do what is right or lawful. So you see, *tzedakah* can be translated as righteousness, but only in the sense that it means to do what is right or lawful.

At best, the word righteousness is only a third of the definition of *tzedakah*. Fully translated *tzedakah* means to act charitably (or generously), to act in loving kindness and to act justly towards your neighbor. (Micah 6:8)

# THE INVITATION TO SEE HIM THROUGH RIGHTESOUNESS

*"As for me, I will see your face in righteousness..."* **Psalm 17:15**

Do you now understand how to seek God's face and how to encounter Him? Simply put, David tells us through one of his many inspired Psalms that doing *tzedakah* or following opportunities to do charitable deeds will cause us to see His face. This is also consistent with what teaches us through the prophet Isaiah: *"I, the LORD, have called you in righteousness, and will hold your hand..." (Isaiah 42:6)*

The word translated "called" in this Scripture found in Isaiah is the Hebrew word *"qara,"* which also means to encounter. So there you have it! If you truly want to encounter God and meet Him, you don't have to die. You don't even have to go off to a mountain top for 40 days and 40 nights in seclusion. All you need to do is pursue opportunities to do good and be a blessing to others. Since that is what God Himself is in pursuit of, this is where and how you will find Him. (Jeremiah 9:24; Psalm 1:6)

So there you have it, if you desire to have an encounter with God and to see His face, that encounter will occur as a result of you being occupied with doing *tzedakah*. Hence, the more you engage in doing good for others, the more you engage God's presence and the more clearly you will see His face.

# THE RELATIONSHIP BETWEEEN REPENTANCE AND RIGHTEOUSNESS

*"... seek My face, and turn from their wicked ways, then I will hear from heaven, and will forgive their sin and heal their land."* (2 Chronicles 7:14)

In the process of *teshuvah*, seeking the face of God (through *tzedakah*) is always found in conjunction with turning from one's wicked ways. The word translated here as "turn" is the Hebrew word *"teshuvah,"* which we defined earlier as not only returning to our place with God, but also allowing God to return to His place within us and among us. This relationship between seeking God's face and turning from wickedness cannot be overlooked because it is not really possible to truly repent and return to our place with God without seeking God's face through *tzedakah*.

If you question that connection simply take a look the ministry of John the Baptist. John's ministry was to call people to repentance in light of the Kingdom of God which was at hand. So let's look at what John encouraged people to do to demonstrate that they had truly repented (or returned to their proper place with God and man).

*"And he went into all the region around Jordan, preaching a baptism of repentance for the remission of sins... Then he said to the multitudes that came out to be baptized by him, 'Brood of vipers! Who warned you to flee from the wrath to come? Therefore bear fruits worthy of repentance, and do not begin to say to yourselves, we have Abraham as our father. For I say to you that God is able to raise up children to Abraham from these stones... So the people asked him saying, what shall we do then?*

*He answered and said to them, He who has two tunics, let him give to him who has none; and he who has food, let him do likewise.'"* (Luke 3:3, 7-8, 10-11)

According to John whose ministry was to prepare the way for the Messiah, it was not enough to simply desire repentance or to be baptized. If there was a true returning in an individual's heart it would be evident in their relationship with their fellow man. So in essence John stated that the seeking to do *tzedakah* (righteousness) was proof of that one had returned to his or her proper place with God. In other words, if you have returned to your place with God and allowed God His rightful place in your heart, you would respond appropriately to the needs and interests of others. Do not be deceived, baptism is not the proof of your repentance. The fact that you move to feed the hungry or clothe the naked, or visit the sick is the evidence that you have achieved the *teshuvah* God desires.

# NOW THE LAND CAN BE HEALED

Once an individual or nation has reached *teshuvah*, healing and restoration are automatically attained. In the face of the shaking of a Shemitah Year, this means we don't need to pray for the economy. It means we don't need to pray that our nation's productivity increase or that our debt be reduced. It means we don't need to pray for healing and the eradication of diseases or pestilence. It means we don't need to ask God to shield us from our enemies who are entering the open doors of our nation. It also means we don't need to pray for better leaders or a better government. All we need to do is seek to *teshuvah*. Once we have arrived at the place of *teshuvah* all of our concerns and anxieties will be eliminated and our nation healed of its afflictions. Everything we need will be added to us. (Matthew 6:33)

How or what should be the prayer of our hearts during a Shemitah Year? How do we pray when God's judgment of our nation seems to be imminent? How should we pray as we strive to humble ourselves and seek the face of God? Earlier as we dissected the process of *teshuvah* according to 2 Chronicles 7:14, we intentionally skipped over the step of prayer. Now we shall direct our attention to the prayer of repentance in a Shemitah Year and the prayer of release.

# CHAPTER 6

# THE IMPACT OF THE PRAYER OF REPENTANCE

*"The Lord is not slack concerning His promise, as some count slackness, but is longsuffering toward us, not willing that any should perish, but that all should come to repentance."* (2 Peter 3:9)

Unfortunately there are many people who do not believe that God will judge the world and His people. Remember the word translated as God, *Elohim*, literally refers to God in the sense of a judge and ruler. When we say the word God, we are speaking of the one and only true Judge. How do people, even Christians, stray and allow themselves to be deceived or forget that there are consequences for our actions? In large part, the answer to that question is revealed in the previous verse. In other words, because God is longsuffering and does not carry out punishment or consequences immediately for our actions, some people are lulled by the enemy into thinking that God does not care and will not judge us accordingly.

We must understand that what is perceived as the delayed response of God is not because there are no consequences to our actions, but because He is allowing time for an individual or nation to repent so that none will perish, but rather return to their place with Him and allow Him to return to His place within and among us.

Fortunately for us, this means we still have time to turn. Even in the seventh year and the year of judgment, we can still humble ourselves, pray and seek God's face and return to Him. Because of God's longsuffering, I don't know if there is such as thing as too late.  Just ask Lazarus. (John 11)  Even if the judgment of God already seems to be in the process of being carried out, you can still pray and seek *teshuvah*.  As matter of fact, I would like to direct your attention to the prayer of Daniel during a time where the children of Israel were under God's judgment.  Interestingly, this prayer of repentance and judgment was due to the fact that Israel had not obeyed God's instructions to observe not just one, but *seventy* Shemitah Years! (Daniel 9:2; Jeremiah 25:1-11)

Consider Daniel's prayer of repentance for the nation, because it had turned from God.  However, before you read this prayer, you need to understand that Daniel's heart was determined to understand why God's people and the nation He loved, was in such turmoil.  Daniel wanted to know where was the prosperity and protection promised to God's people?  What sin(s) had they committed as a nation that would cause God to turn His back on Israel?  It was this desire to diagnose the cause which led Daniel to study the writings of the prophet Jeremiah where he found both the cause and the solution. (Daniel 9:2)

# DANIEL'S PRAYER OF REPENTANCE FOR THE NATION

*"In the first year of Darius the son of Ahasuerus, of the lineage of the Medes, who was made king over the realm of the Chaldeans- in the first year of his reign I Daniel understood by books the number of the years specified by the word of the LORD through Jeremiah the prophet, that He would accomplish seventy years in the desolations of Jerusalem.*

*Then I set my face toward the Lord my God, and made confession, and said, O Lord, great and awesome God, who keeps His covenant and mercy with those who love Him, and with those who keep His commandments, we have sinned and committed iniquity, we have done wickedly and rebelled, even by departing from Your precepts and Your judgments. Neither have we heeded Your servants the prophets, who spoke in Your name to our kings and our princes, to our fathers and all the people of the land. O Lord, righteousness belongs to You, but to us shame of face, as it is this day – to the men of Judah, to the inhabitants of Jerusalem and all Israel, those near and those far off in all the countries to which You have driven them, because of the unfaithfulness which they have committed against You.*

*O Lord, to us belongs shame of face, to our kings, our princes and our father, because we have sinned against You. To the Lord our God belong mercy and forgiveness, though we have rebelled against Him. We have not obeyed the voice of the LORD our God, to walk in His laws, which He set before us by His servants the prophets.*

*Yes, all Israel has transgressed Your law, and has departed so as not to obey Your voice; therefore the curse and the oath written in the Law of Moses the servant of God have been poured out on us, because we have sinned against Him. And he has confirmed His words, which He spoke against us and against our judges who judged us, by bringing upon us a great disaster; for under the whole heaven such has never been done as what has been done to Jerusalem.*

*As it is written in the Law of Moses, all this disaster has come upon us; yet we have not made our prayer before the LORD our God, that we might turn from our iniquities and understand Your truth. Therefore the LORD has kept the disaster in mind, and brought it*

*upon us; for the LORD our God is righteous in all the works which*
*He does, though we have not obeyed His voice.*

*And now, O Lord our God, who brought Your people out of the land*
*of Egypt with a mighty hand, and made Yourself a name as it is this*
*day – we have sinned, we have done wickedly! O Lord, according*
*to all Your righteousness, I pray, let Your anger and Your fury be*
*turned away from Your city Jerusalem, Your holy mountain;*
*because for our sins and for the iniquities of our fathers, Jerusalem*
*and Your people are a reproach to all those around us.*

*Now therefore, our God, hear the prayer of Your servant, and his*
*supplications, and for the Lord's sake cause Your face to shine on*
*Your sanctuary, which is desolate. O my God, incline Your ear and*
*hear; open Your eyes and see our desolations, and the city which is*
*called by Your name; for we do not present our supplications*
*before Your because of our righteous deeds, but because of Your*
*great mercies. O Lord, hear! O Lord, forgive! O Lord listen and*
*act! Do not delay for Your own sake, my God, for Your city and*
*Your people are called by Your name."* (Daniel 9:1-19)

# DISECTING DANIEL'S PRAYER

As we analyze Daniel's prayer to see if we can better understand
the prayer of *teshuvah*, we must first remember that Daniel was
not as moved by the calamity and desolation of his people, as
much as he was stirred by the nation having moved away from
God. (Daniel 9:5)  It was the realization that they had sinned
against the God who had been so faithful and gracious to them
that moved him to repentance for the nation.  Daniel possessed a
sense and feeling of deep shame because of how Israel had
disobeyed God and brought dishonor upon His Holy Name.  From

this context, we can conclude that one of the requirements necessary before one can offer a true prayer of repentance is a deep sense of shame.

# IT'S NOT ENOUGH TO BE SORRY

What does it mean to experience the sense of shame Daniel experienced? Is shame and sorrow the same thing? Is shame really necessary for repentance? These are questions that we shall now answer. What does the scripture say about sorrow in relation to repentance? Look at what the apostle Paul says about the matter:

*"For godly sorrow produces repentance leading to salvation, not to be regretted; but the sorrow of the world produces death. For observe this very thing,that you sorrowed in a godly manner: What diligence it produced in you, what clearing of yourselves, what indignation, what fear, what vehement desire, what zeal, what vindication! In all things you proved yourselves to be clear in this matter"* (2 Corinthians 7:10-11)

As we examine this Scripture we see the apostle Paul explaining that worldly sorrow does not lead to repentance, but death. This is because worldly sorrow is simply sadness that an individual may experience because of their external condition. In other words, worldly sorrow is not motivated by the internal state and actions of an individual or nation. It is the state of being unhappy with one's environment. In this state there is no regret for the thoughts and actions of one's heart, which resulted in desolation, only remorse for what has happened.

# SHAME IS BETTER FOR REPENTANCE THAN SORROW

This type of (worldly) sorrow is starkly contrasted with godly sorrow, which leads to true repentance. According to the apostle Paul, godly sorrow is depicted as a sense of guilt and shame not only for one's state of being, but a sense of shame for the thoughts of their heart and actions. This is the idea expressed by Daniel through his prayer of repentance, a feeling of shame in appearance before God and man.

The world translated as "shame" in Daniel 9:7, is the Hebrew word *"bosheth"*, which is from the root word *"bush"*. This word was first used in Genesis 2:25 where it was stated that Adam and his wife were both naked and not <u>ashamed</u>.

However, in the next chapter we see that they were no longer unashamed of their nakedness and attempted to cover themselves. (Genesis 3:7-8) This first account of the word and idea of shame as found in Genesis, helps us to understand the shame one must feel before true repentance can be attained. A person without shame feels no need to hide or cover up anything. However, when a person feels shame they feel a need to hide and improve themselves. This is evident in the fact that Adam and Eve tried to improve their appearance by covering themselves with fig leaves.

# THE STENCH OF SHAME

Although I think we have accurately defined the idea of being ashamed, we can still give a clearer and more functional description of the word. Interestingly, the word *"bosheth"* (shame) is related to the word *"beosh"*, which refers to something that gives off a stench or a loathsome odor. This is the kind of foul odor that can make others nauseous and even sick to their stomach (and vomit). For example, the stench of a skunk is *"beosh"* or loathsome among animals. Its odor keeps other animals away and at a great distance and it represents the idea of shame in a very concrete way.

This is the type of shame expressed by Daniel in his prayer of repentance. A feeling of having done something so embarrassing and abhorrent that he felt like God would remain at a distance to keep from being contaminated with such an odor. The type of shame Daniel possessed was a feeling God would be defiling himself and tarnishing His holiness to be in fellowship with Israel after all they had done. To be sure, this is the type of shame one experiences before true and genuine *teshuvah* can be achieved.

By the way before we examine more the category of a prayer of repentance, I thought you would be grateful and thankful to know that Yeshua is the evidence that God is more than willing to experience shame and rejection in order to resume fellowship with man. Here is what God said through the prophet Isaiah about His willingness to endure shame for us: *"I gave my back to those who struck Me, and My checks to those who plucked out the beard; I did not hide My face from shame and spitting."* (Isaiah 50:6) There is still hope!

# THE RIGHT KIND OF PRAYER FOR REPENTANCE

In Scripture there are several words for prayer as there are several types of prayers that one may offer. So when examining the type of prayers offered in Scripture you need specifically identify the word translated as prayer at each instance. The word God uses in 2 Chronicles 7:14 to identify the type of prayer which is necessary for repentance is *"palal"*. This word *palal* is a word for prayer, which means to intercede with a judge in hopes of a more favorable outcome. The Hebrew letters which form the world *palal* creates a pictograph of someone coming to speak with an authority or judge. It is the idea of speaking to one who has the authority and power to decide the future of another.

The first mention of this type of prayer is found in Genesis 20 after Abimelech took Abraham's wife Sarah. Take a look at the Scripture to see the role *palal* (prayer) played in keeping Abimilech from death.

*"Now Abraham said of Sarah his wife, she is my sister. And Abimelech king of Gerar sent and took Sarah... And God said to him in a dream, yes I know that you did this in the integrity of your heart. For I also withheld you from sinning against Me; therefore I did not let you touch her. Now therefore, __restore__ the man's wife; for he is a prophet, and he will __pray__ for you and you shall live. But if you do not restore her, know that you shall surely die, you and all who are yours... Then Abimelech took sheep, oxen, and male and female servants, and gave them to Abraham; and he restored Sarah his wife to him... So Abraham __prayed__ to God; and God healed Abimelech, his wife, and his female servants. Then they bore children; for the LORD had closed up all the wombs of the*

*house of Abimelech because of Sarah, Abraham's wife."* (Genesis 20:2, 6-7, 14, 17-18 *emphasis added)

In examining this passage we can better understand the role of *palal* in *teshuvah* (or the role of prayer in repentance). After Abimelech had taken Sarah, God appeared to him in a dream and instructed him to "restore" Sarah to her husband. Interestingly, the word translated restore is *"shuv"* the root of *teshuvah*, a word that means to return. So we see that Abimelech is in need of repentance or returning someone, namely Sarah, to the place God had purposed for her.

Secondly, God tells Abimelech that if he does not return Sarah to her place that he and his entire household would die. Later, we find out that Abimelech and his household had already been afflicted, by God because he removed Sarah from her place. (Genesis 20:18) However, it doesn't end there. God also told Abimelech that if he returned Sarah to her place that Abraham would pray for him and that he would live. As you probably already guessed the word translated prayer is *"palal,"* and in this context it implies that Abraham would plead with God the Judge on behalf of Abimelech. It also meant that Abraham would act as Abimelech's attorney and seek a more favorable judgment for him.

# MOSES'S PRAYER OF REPENTANCE SAVED THE NATION OF ISRAEL FROM DESTRUCTION

At this point we have examined Daniel's prayer of repentance for the nation of Israel, while in Babylonian captivity. On a more personal note we reviewed how Abraham's prayer brought healing to a king in need of repentance.  Now I would like to show you how Moses' prayer helped to save the nation of Israel from destruction after they had committed the grave sin of making and worshiping a golden calf.

*"Then the LORD said to me, arise, go down quickly from here, for your people whom you brought out of Egypt have acted corruptly; <u>they have quickly turned aside from the way which I have commanded them</u>; they have made themselves a molded image.  Furthermore, the LORD spoke to me, saying, I have seen this people, and indeed they are a stiff-necked people.  Let Me alone, that I may destroy them and blot out their name from under heaven; and I will make of you a nation mightier and greater than they...*

*And I fell down before the LORD, as at the first forty days and forty nights; I neither ate bread nor drank water, because of all your sins which you committed in doing wickedly in the sight of the LORD, to provoke His anger.  For I was afraid of the anger and hot displeasure with which the LORD was angry with you, to destroy you.  But the LORD listened to me at that time also...  Therefore I prayed to the LORD, and said O Lord God, do not destroy Your people and Your inheritance whom You have redeemed through Your greatness, whom You have brought out of Egypt with a mighty hand.  Remember Your servants, Abraham, Isaac and Jacob; do not look on the stubbornness of this people, or on their wickedness or their sin, lest the land from which You brought us should say, because the LORD was not able to bring them to the land which He promised them, and because He hated the, He has brought them out to kill them in the wilderness.*

*Yet they are Your people and Your inheritance, whom You brought out by Your mighty power and by Your outstretched arm...As at* *the first time, I stayed in the mountain forty days and forty nights;* <u>*the LORD also heard me at that time, and the LORD chose not to*</u> <u>*destroy you.*</u> *Then the LORD said to me, arise, begin your journey before the people that they may go in and possess the land which I swore to their fathers to give them."* (Deuteronomy 9:12-14, 18,19, 26-29; 10:10,11 *emphasis added)

# THE CALL OF AN ADVOCATE

As in the last two examples with both Daniel and Abraham, the word translated as prayer in the previous passage of Scripture is also *"palal."* In this passage had Moses not pleaded with the Judge on behalf of Israel, they would have been destroyed. Again, we see that there is hope for even a nation who angers God. God does not want to see His people destroyed; therefore, He is longsuffering and merciful.

As a matter of fact, whenever an individual or nation strays too far away from their place with God, He begins searching for a man or woman to *"palal"* or plead with Him on their behalf. (Ezekiel 22:30) He looks for a person who will be an advocate for those guilty of breaking God's laws. He wants someone who may even be willing to make some sort of personal sacrifice to save an individual or nation from God's judgment. Yeshua (Jesus) is that kind of person!

Not only was Yeshua the perfect example of an advocate for a people in need of repentance, but He was even willing to make the ultimate sacrifice of His own life to save others from God's judgment. In the final and last chapter, we will examine how the ministry of Yeshua and those who follow His teachings and example are the answer and hope of those facing the judgment of a Shemitah Year.

# CHAPTER 7

# HOW TO POSITION YOURSELF IN A SHEMITAH YEAR

*"For He says: In an acceptable time I have heard you, and in the day of salvation I have helped you. Behold, now is the accepted time; behold, now is the day of salvation." (2 Corinthians 6:2)*

Do you know of anyone who truly has a heart and compassion which moves them to stand in the gap for others? Someone who is more interested in pointing the way to safety than in condemning others? Who is willing to make a personal sacrifice if necessary to help save others? Who believes both repentance and salvation can be achieved today? If you are a follower of Yeshua the Messiah, you should know many who fit this description. The entire ministry of Yeshua and His followers was to carry out *teshuvah* (in the sense of returning mankind to his place with God). Look at how Apostle Paul describes the ministry of Yeshua and that of His followers.

*"Now all things are of God, who has reconciled us to Himself through Jesus Christ, and has given us the ministry of reconciliation, that is, that God was in Christ reconciling the world to Himself, not imputing their trespasses to them, and has committed to us the word of reconciliation. Now then we are ambassadors for Christ, as though God were pleading through us: we implore you on Christ's behalf, be reconciled to God. For He made Him who knew no sin to be sin for us, that we might become the righteousness of God in Him. We then, as workers together with Him, also plead with you not to receive the grace of God in vain." (2 Corinthians 5:18-6:1 \*emphasis added)*

# THE MINISTRY OF RECONCILATION IS A MINISTRY OF TESHUVAH

Five times in the previous passage of Scripture, various forms of the word "reconcile" are used to describe the ministry of Yeshua and His followers as having a ministry of reconciliation. If nothing else, from this passage we should understand what word best describes what should be the primary work of followers of Yeshua. But what does it mean to be reconciled? The English word reconciled is from the Latin word *reconcilliare,* to bring together again. As such, reconciliation occurs when two or more parties who were at one time estranged from one another are brought together in unity and harmony again.

Does that sound familiar? If it sounds a lot like *teshuvah,* that's because the purpose of the ministry of reconciliation is to bring about *teshuvah.* Remember, *teshuvah* is a word that describes one returning to their place with God and allowing God to return to his place within and among His people.

# THE FUNCTION OF AMBASSADORS OF CHRIST

Often times you may hear people refer to themselves or others as ambassadors of Christ. What does it mean to be an ambassador of Christ? According to 2 Corinthians 5:20, being an ambassador of Christ means that one has been given the task of reconciling others to God. Their primary goal or objective is not to get people to return to their place in church, but to return to their place of purpose with God.

An ambassador for Christ is also equipped with the word of reconciliation. This means that they speak and teach others about God's desire for them to return to their place with Him. They help others to understand that outside of God they are like a fish out of water. Moreover, with Him is the abundant life that they were meant for. The Scripture teaches us that Heaven rejoices when just one person is returned to their place with God. (Luke 15:6The true ambassadors of Christ create opportunities for rejoicing in Heaven. When was the last time you encouraged someone to return to their place with God? Is it important to you to see individuals and nations returned to God?

# REPENT OR ELSE...

Knowing now that we have been called to the ministry of reconciliation and that the purpose of reconciliation is repentance (or returning people to their place with God), read the following Scriptures. This passage shows the role of the repentance in the ministry of reconciliation, which we have been given.

- *"In those days John the Baptist came preaching in the wilderness of Judea, and saying, 'Repent, for the Kingdom of Heaven is at hand!'"* (Matthew 3:1-2)

- *"From that time Jesus began to preach and to say, 'Repent for the Kingdom of Heaven is at hand.'"* (Matthew 4:17)

- *"So they went out and preached that people should repent."* (Mark 6:12)

- *"Take heed to yourselves. If your brother sins against you, rebuke him; and if he repents, forgive him."* (Luke 17:3)

- *"Repent therefore of this your wickedness, and pray God if perhaps the thought of your heart may be forgiven."* (Acts 8:22)

- *Truly, these times of ignorance God overlooked, but now commands all men everywhere to repent,"* (Acts 17:30)

- *"And I gave her time to repent of her sexual immorality, and she did not repent. Indeed I will cast her into a bed, and those who commit adultery with her into great tribulation, unless they repent of their deeds."* (Revelation 2:21-22)

- *"There were present at that season some who told Him about the Galileans whose blood Pilate had mingled with their sacrifices. And Jesus answered and said to them, Do you suppose that these Galileans were worse sinners than all other Galileans, because they suffered such things? I tell you, no; but unless you repent you will all likewise perish. Or those eighteen on whom the tower in Siloam fell and killed them, do you think that they were worse sinners than all other men who dwelt in Jerusalem? I tell you, no; but unless you repent you will all likewise perish."* (Luke 13:1-5)

According to the teaching of Scripture, we need to understand that unless there is repentance, destruction is certain. Once we comprehend this, we realize that we cannot be sluggish about helping people to be reconciled and returned to their place with God. Time is not necessarily on our side in this matter. Particularly due the fact that we are in a Shemitah Year, we should have a greater sense of urgency to bring about reconciliation. Remember, the Shemitah Year is a time when shaking and collapse occurs. Throughout history, individuals and nations have fallen due to the shaking and judgment carried out as a result of a Shemitah. Therefore, we must be watchful and take advantage of every opportunity to strengthen those that are weak and dying.

*"Be watchful, and strengthen the things which remain, that are ready to die: for I have not found your works perfect before God. Remember therefore how you have received and heard; hold fast and repent. Therefore if you will not watch, I will come upon you as a thief, and you will not know what hour I will come upon you."* (Revelation 3:2-3)

# BEING A DESTROYER WATCHER

If you are a true follower of Yeshua, then the idea of being watchful and vigilant in strengthening the weak should resonate in your soul. This is due to the fact that Yeshua Himself was the greatest advocate of the weak and broken. This was not only His ministry, but delivering people from harm and danger was His actual identity and name.

As we stated in the beginning of this book, Jesus' Hebrew name is Yeshua and it means a savior or deliverer. However, there is more we can glean from His name when we look deeper. The root word of Yeshua is the word *"yasha"*, spelled with the following Hebrew letters. The *yod* (י) is a picture of the hand and represents work. The *shin* (שׁ) is a picture of teeth and is a picture of consuming, destroying or destroyer. The *ayin* (ע) is a picture of an eye and represents watching. Combined, this means that **Yeshua (and or salvation) is a picture of one** working as a destroyer watcher (or one working to watch for the destroyer).

# WILL YOU BE A WATCHMAN FOR THE LORD?

*"Son of man, I have made you a watchman for the house of Israel: therefore hear a word from My mouth, and give them warning from Me."* (Ezekiel 3:17)

The pictograph of Yeshua's name does not just mean His function is to watch over God's people (John 10:11-16), but that He actively guards and protects His flock against things that could potentially destroy them.  It does not matter if the potential destroyer is sickness, famine, poverty, sin, etc.  Therefore the Scripture says, *"...For this purpose the Son of God was manifested, that He might destroy the works of the devil."* (1 John 3:8b)

Here is an interesting thought and a question.  We who believe on Yeshua are supposed to be followers of His life and example, right?  So if Yeshua functioned as a destroyer watcher, then shouldn't those who follow Him, watch over and guard their neighbors for potential destroyers?  Furthermore, if His ministry work was to deliver and rescue people from potential destroyers, then shouldn't we also seek to rescue people from potential destroyers?  If your answer to those questions is yes, then you should also seek to help people repent from paths that lead to destruction and return to their place with God, where they will find safety and salvation.

God is currently looking for those would stand in the gap and plead for the safety and welfare of those in danger of judgment.

(Ezekiel 22:30) We are in the midst of a Shemitah Year and a game changing event is likely on the horizon and most people are ignorant of where the nation is headed. Carefully consider the Word of the LORD to those He has appointed as watchmen.

*"When I say to the wicked, you shall surely die, and you give him no warning, nor speak to warn the wicked form his wicked way, to save his life, that same wicked man shall die in his iniquity; but his blood I will require at your hand. Yet if you warn the wicked and he does not turn from his wickedness, nor from his wicked way he shall die in his iniquity; but you have delivered your soul."* (Ezekiel 3:18-19)

# IT'S TIME TO WATCH AND PRAY

*"Watch therefore and pray always that you may be counted worthy to escape all these things that will come to pass, and to stand before the Son of Man."* (Luke 21:36)

If you are serious about seeing the nation(s) returned to God and saved from judgment and calamity during this Shemitah Year, then you must be a person given to prayer. The majority of our opposition and struggle is not against things that we can see or things that are tangible. According to the Scripture the real struggle we face is against spiritual wickedness in high places; against powers and principalities. (Ephesians 6:12) There are spiritual enemies of our nation that will not be defeated by a simple vote or change in political parties. These are enemies that seek to destroy our nations from the top down. They are enemies that will not give up their intent to destroy the nation(s) because its people store food, water and invest in gold and silver.

While I appreciate the intent of talk radio and the media to inform the people of what is happening and how it will affect the people, the answer is not to spin or politicize the news events of the day. If you listen to the news and various media outlets, you should have a current working prayer list. It's not enough just to discuss the intent of leaders and their policies, if we will not **COMMIT** these topics to prayer. Look at what the Scripture says about the need for followers of Yeshua to pray for the government.

*"Therefore I exhort first of all that supplications, prayers, intercessions and giving of thanks be made for all men, for kings and all who are in authority, that we may lead a quiet and peaceable life in all godliness and reverence. For this is good and acceptable in the sight of God our Savior, who desires all men to be saved and to come to the knowledge of the truth."* (1 Timothy 2:1-4)

From this Scripture understand that God wants us to pray for all men. Not just for those we know and love, but for ALL mankind, and for those in leadership on all levels. As a matter of fact, we are also taught in this passage that the peace of individuals and nations is directly related to the prayers, supplications and intercession of God's people. If there is prosperity and peace it is a sign that prayers are being offered. If there is decline or calamity and a decrease in peace, it is an indicator that prayers have been lacking.

# UNLEASH THE POWER OF PRAYER

If you want to see peace and stability in your nation's government, pray. Make supplications and intercession on behalf of your government. If you want to see peace and stability in your nation's economy, pray. Make supplications and intercession on behalf of business or marketplace leaders and workers. If you want to see peace and stability in your nation's families or education system, pray. Make supplication and intercession on their behalf.

In his inspired wisdom King Solomon reminded us of God's power even over the leaders of nations and that He can redirect and guide our nation's leaders as we pray. (Proverbs 21:1) Please do not be deceived! The prayers of God's people are not impotent or just some vain and ineffective religious act. The prayers of God's people can shake the heavens and put the enemies of our nations to flight. Regardless of how ordinary or insignificant a person may appear, God has a thing for using things that appear weak and foolish to confound the enemy. Look at what the Scripture says about how an ordinary man like Elijah influenced a nation to repent and overthrew principalities and powers.

*"Confess your trespasses to one another, and pray for one another, that you may be healed, the effective, fervent prayer of a righteous man avails much. Elijah was a man with a nature like ours, and he prayed earnestly that it would not rain; and it did not rain on the land for three years and six months. And he prayed again, and the heaven gave rain, and the earth produced its fruit."* (James 5:16-18)

# BE COMMITTED TO PRAYER

We can no longer afford to be doubtful or negligent in the area of prayer. If you want to see a change in your nation, ask for it. If you have already asked, ask again, and again and again. Remember God has called to you offer *"palal"* (prayers). In the same way that a defense attorney continues to make his case before the Judge, you continue to make your case to God on behalf of the nation(s). Not only is there power in your prayer to influence the Judge and the heavens, but through you, God is able to do exceedingly and abundantly above and beyond what you think of as possible. (Ephesians 3:20)

From this point forward, as a watchman you should set regular times for prayer. You should have a prayer journal in which you keep a current prayer list and record of prayers that have been answered. Pray with expectation, believing that God not only hears you, but that He desires to hear from you. Pray believing that God wants to save the nation and help them avoid calamity more than you or anyone in your nation. Lastly, you should pray from your heart. If you don't feel the significance of the words you are praying, you are wasting your time. What sense does it make to try and move heaven with things that don't move you? Which is easier to move heaven and earth, or you? When you are moved with compassion and offer prayers, then Heaven can also be moved.

# BEING AN EMISSARY OF THE LORDS RELEASE

*"At the end of every seven years you shall grant a release of debts... because it is called the LORD's release."* (Deuteronomy 15:1, 2b)

Earlier we discussed the fact that the Shemitah Year is also referred to as the year of release. However, this release is not about God releasing us, as much as it is about God directing us to release others from debt. I would like to resume our investigation of what it means to release others in this year of release. We'll start with a reminder of the meaning of the word translated as "debt," which is the word *"neshiy"*.

While a *neshiy* can refer to a monetary debt, it more specifically refers to a continuous pressure or burden. Regardless of where it comes from or the level of stress it causes, if it results in a person feeling constant pressure, it can be described as a *"neshiy."*

In a Shemitah Year God especially commissions His people to release others from burdens and pressure. This is the LORD's release in every sense of the word, so it is not us who are even required to do the majority of the heavy lifting. God Himself is simply looking for those through whom He can work to lift heavy burdens and destroy yokes. (Matthew 11:28-30)

Interestingly, when Yeshua taught His disciples to pray, He included a portion of prayer that was equivalent to the idea of releasing others from burdens and debts during the seventh year. Let's look at this prayer which incorporates the idea of releasing others from *neshiy*.

# PRAYING TO THE LORD FOR RELEASE

*"In this manner, therefore, pray: Our Father in heaven, hallowed be Your name. Your Kingdom come. Your Will be done on earth as it is in heaven. Give us this day our daily bread. And **forgive us our debts, as we forgive our debtors**. And do not lead us into*

*temptation, but deliver us from the evil one. For yours is the Kingdom and the power and the glory forever. Amen.* ***For if you forgive men their trespasses, your heavenly Father will also forgive you. But if you do not forgive men their trespasses, neither will your Father forgive your trespasses.***" (Matthew 6:9-15 *emphasis added)

Do you see the connection between this prayer and the release of the Shemitah Year? In this prayer, Yeshua teaches His disciples that the Father will forgive their debts, to the degree that they forgive the debts of others. Obviously, we would gain a better understanding of what is being communicated here if we insert the Hebrew idea and concept of debt. When you plug the idea of *neshiy* for debt, you see that Yeshua is teaching His disciples to forgive the continuous pressure and burdens of others and God will forgive their burdens.

Does this make sense to you? In western thought it doesn't really make sense to forgive someone for having burdens. So, plug in the Hebrew word and meaning of forgive and see if it makes a little more sense.

Remarkably, one of the Hebrew words translated as "forgive" is actually related to the word translated as "debt." The word for debt is *"neshiy"* and the word "forgive" is *"nasa"*. If you look at the Hebrew letters you can actually see that these two words have the same root letters of *nun* (נ) and *shin* (שׁ). So what does it mean to *"nasa"* someone's *"neshiy"* or to forgive someone's debt? The word *nasa* does means to forgive, but it also means to lift up a burden or a load and to carry it. Put more plainly, *nasa* (or to forgive in the mind of God) means to lift up and bear someone else's burden.

Now when you read the prayer Yeshua taught His disciples you can understand it is better interpreted and understood as follows:

*"Our Father in heaven, hallowed be Your name. Your kingdom come. Your will be done on earth as it is in heaven. Give us this day our daily bread, and* <u>**lift up, carry and even remove our burdens, as we lift up, carry and remove the burdens of others.**</u> (Matthew 6:9-12)

# BEING YOKED TO YESHUA

What a powerful and applicable definition of how God wants us forgive others! God wants us to release others from their constant pressures. He wants us to lift up and carry the burdens that others are under especially during a Shemitah Year, the year of the LORD'S release. This should be at the very heart of our prayers and desires during Shemitah Year. The Father removes burdens and destroys yokes and that we also strive to, at the very least, make others burdens lighter.

As followers of Yeshua, we must remember that He Himself invited those who were burdened to come to Him so He could carry their burdens (Matthew 11:28-30). That means as His followers, we should also extend this same invitation to those under the stress and pressures of life. Don't be afraid or hesitant, because you feel inadequate or lacking in ability to aid others. Remember, that Yeshua not only invited us to bring our burdens to Him, He also offered us the opportunity to be yoked to Him. If you understood this metaphor of being yoked to Yeshua, you would understand not only how He helps with your burdens, but how He will help us to carry the burdens of theirs.

# YESHUA IS THE STRONG OX

*"Take My yoke upon you and learn fro me..."* (Matthew 11:29)

In ancient Israel a farmer would often put a younger (weaker) and less experienced ox together in a yoke with an older, much stronger and more experienced ox. As a result, the younger ox would not only learn how to plow and carry a burden, but it would also be able to rest as the stronger ox carried the majority of the load. For us Yeshua is the Strong Ox. He lifts the weight of our burdens and carries them for us and in doing so He also shows us how to help others carry their burdens. Especially in this Shemitah Year, God is calling you to be the stronger ox for someone who is weaker. As the year progresses, you will see that the need and call to be a burden bearer will increase. If you accept this call not only will you be emulating Yeshua as a deliverer, but you will be functioning as a watchman for God's people.

God has also reserved a special blessing for those who seek to obey His call to free others during this Shemitah Year. Not only has God promised that if you relieve others of their burdens that he would relieve you of yours, but He has stated that to the degree and measure with which you release others, He will release you.

*"Give, and it will be given to you; good measure, press down, shaken together and running over will be put into your bosom. For with the same measure that you use, it will be measure back to you."* (Luke 6:38)

# GOD'S PROMISE FOR RELEASING OTHERS

God has promised to match your efforts towards others. In other words, in a Shemitah Year, when you become an advocate for others (relieving their burdens and saving them from destruction) God will remove your burdens and save you as well. Remember you are living in a nation that is likely to face God's judgment. If the economy fails, if there is war, or if a disease pandemic is on the horizon, will you just be happy you have on a life vest? Instead, will you try to make sure others are safe as well?

Now, there is more to God's promise for those who help others in need during a Shemitah Year. Not only has God promised that He would help you as you help others, but He has promised that He will abundantly bless you and bless the work of your hands, so that you increase greatly. Take a look below.

*"At the end of every seven years you shall grant a release of debts. And this is the form of the release: Every creditor who has lent anything to his neighbor shall release it; he shall not require it of his neighbor or his brother, because it is called the LORD'S release...Only if you carefully obey the voice of the LORD your God, to observe with care all these commandments which I command you today. For the LORD your God will bless you just as He promised you; you shall lend to many nations, but you shall not borrow; you shall reign over many nations, but they shall not reign over you.*

*If there is among you a poor man of your brethren, within any of the gates in your land which the LORD your God is giving you, you shall not harden your heart nor shut your hand from your poor*

*brother, but you shall open your hand wide to him and willingly*
*lend him sufficient for his need whatever he needs... You shall*
*surely give to him, and your heart should not be grieved when you*
*give to him, because for this thing the LORD your God will bless you*
*in all your works and in all to which you put your hand."*
(Deuteronomy 15:1,2; 5-8, 10)

# WILL YOU BE PART OF THE SHEMITAH SOLUTION?

This passage in Deuteronomy outlines the promise of God for
granting a release of debts and burdens of others during a
Shemitah Year. God wants to relieve you of your burdens. He
wants to bless the works of your hands and prosper you in all
you do. He wants to save your city and nation from economic
collapse and calamity, and He wants to see individuals and
nations returned to their place with Him. You are a key to God's
plan for releasing blessing and prosperity over our cities and
nations. You have the power and opportunity to grant a release
of God's salvation, protection and blessing over your family,
community and nation. God is calling for you to be an emissary
of His release. He wants you to be a vessel through whom He
will remove burdens and destroy yokes. Will you be the
watchman and burden remover God is calling for? Will you be
the answer to the shaking of this Shemitah Year?

# GLOSSARY

*Ot* (אות) a miraculous sign, or an unusual occurrence or event

*Eth* (עת): important *times*, but also a pictograph of seeing or watching for the signs of the covenant.

**Binyah** (בינה): Understanding

*Bosheth* (בשת), shame

*Beosh* (באש): something that gives off a stench or a loathsome odor

*Chagab* (חגב): a locust

*Dabar* (דבר): spoken word, or to communicate with.

*Deber* (דבר): pestilence

*Kana* (כנע): submission, to be submissive

*Kalah* (כלה): the end and completion of a thing

*Mashach* ( משח): to be anointed

*Moed* (מועד): (or *moedim* in the plural sense) and it refers to divinely appointed times and seasons.

*Moshiach* (משיח): the Messiah

*Nasa* (נשא): to forgive, to lift up a burden or a load and to carry it, or to bear someone else's burden

*Navi* (נבא): Prophet; or prophesy; also a pictograph of that which is housed in a seed, or fruit

**Neshiy** (נְשִׁי): something owed often with interest, also a picture of a continuous pressure on someone

**Palal** (פלל): prayer, to intercede with a judge in hopes of a more favorable outcome on behalf of oneself or another

**Shabath** (שַׁבַּת): to rest

**Shebee** (שְׁבַעִי): seven

**Shemitah** (שמטה): a remission of debt or a suspension of labor, also means to throw down or a shaking

**Shuv or Teshuvah** (שׁוּב): repentance, or returning to ones place with God

**Tzedakah** (צדקה): righteousness, to act charitably (or generously), to act in loving kindness and to act justly towards your neighbor.

**Yeshua** (יֵשׁע): savior, deliverer, a one who is a destroyer watcher

**Zeman** (זמן): appointed occasions and seasons

# Other Books by Anderick Biddle

## Kingdom Treasury Volume 1: Unleashing The Power of Ancient Tzedakah Mysteries

# One Last Thing

Your feedback and comments would be greatly appreciated. Oftentimes your feedback is instrumental in further developing this book or other writings. If you'd like to leave a review, please visit Amazon or click here in your ebook.

Thanks again for your support!

CPSIA information can be obtained at www.ICGtesting.com
Printed in the USA
LVOW10s1423070615

441504LV00037B/1447/P